Beardie Basics

Beginner's Guide to Bearded Collies

Barbara Hagen Rieseberg
and
Betty J. McKinney

With Contributions by
Jo Parker

Alpine
Blue Ribbon Books

Alpine Publications, P.O. Box 7027, Loveland, CO 80537

BEARDIE BASICS: Beginner's Guide to Bearded Collies

ISBN: 0-931866-99-5

Also by the authors: *Sheltie Talk,* Alpine Publications, 1976, 1985.

Alpine books are available to clubs, organizations, and breeders for premiums and fund-raising at special discounts. For information write to the attention of the Special Markets Director, Alpine Publications, at the above address.

Edited by: Dianne Nelson
Design and layout: Shadow Canyon Graphics, Golden, Colorado
Cover design: B. J. McKinney

Front Photo by Chet Jezierski, courtesy Jo Parker.

1 2 3 4 5 6 7 8 9
Printed in the United States of America

Contents

About the Authors

A longstanding friendship between the authors began in the late 1960s, and together they traveled to Great Britain in 1977 to research the first edition of *Beardie Basics* and to purchase breeding stock.

The authors' first book, *Sheltie Talk*, published in 1967, was conceived because they wanted to give the Sheltie fancier a badly needed source of basic information specific to the breed— information which the authors had difficulty obtaining during their early years as breeders. The book has since become the most widely recommended work on the Shetland Sheepdog.

Barbara Hagen began breeding Shelties in 1961, at the age of fourteen. Over the next sixteen years she bred or owned a dozen champions in Shelties and various other working breeds. In 1970, Barbara married Freedo Rieseberg, who previously had been involved in breeding German Shepherd dogs, and the two continued breeding and showing under her kennel name, Silverleaf. They obtained their first Bearded Collies from England in 1973, with the help of international judge Margaret Osborne, and went on to produce numerous champion and ROM Beardies. In April of 1980, Barbara Rieseberg died—a great loss not only to Freedo, but to the Beardie world as well. Silverleaf Kennel has since become inactive.

B.J. McKinney began breeding and showing Shelties in 1966, under the name Kinni Kennels. Her interest in publications dates back to her twelfth year of age when, with camera and pen, she put together her first "book," a story about a litter of Sheltie puppies. She has been involved in publishing since 1974, and has bred several champion Shetland sheepdogs.

Jo Parker has been a breeder/exhibitor of Bearded Collies since 1974, and is also a licensed AKC judge. Her Parcana kennel has produced many champions, including Best in Show and Group winners. Prior to her involvement with Bearded Collies, she bred Shetland Sheepdogs for nearly thirty years. She is a former President of BCCA, was breed columnist for the *AKC Gazette* for many years, and has written numerous articles. She holds a B.A. in journalism from the University of Alabama.

Presented to

_____,

owner of (dog's registered name):_____.

(Call name)_____ came to live with us on _____,

His/her breeder's name and address is _____

_____

Phone number: home (   ) _____ other (   ) _____.

PERMANENT RECORDS

Sire (father):_____

Dam (mother):_____

Litter Registration No.:_____ Individual No.:_____

Color:_____

IMMUNIZATION RECORD:

1st Puppy DHL Shot   Given by _____   Date_____

Booster DHLP Due _____   Given by _____   Date_____

DHLP Booster Due _____   Given by_____   Date _____

First Rabies Shot Due____   Given by_____   Date_____

Adult Rabies Shot Due___   Given by_____   Date_____

Other Immunizations:_____

_____

WORMING RECORD:

Date_____   Medication_____   By_____

Date_____   Medication_____   By_____

Date_____   Medication_____   By_____

FEEDING RECORDS

When I purchased my dog his food ration was (brand)_____

amount _____ fed _____ times daily.

On _____ his ration was changed to (brand) _____

amount _____ fed _____ times daily.

On _____ his ration was changed to (brand) _____

amount _____ fed _____ times daily.

MEDICAL RECORDS

My veterinarian is

_____

address_____

phone number_____ Emergency number _____

My dog's initial visit was on _____.

Followup visits:

Date_____ Reason_____

Treatment or
notes:_____

Date_____ Reason_____

Treatment or
notes:_____

Date_____ Reason_____

Treatment or
notes:_____

Date_____ Reason_____

Treatment or
notes:_____

TRAINING RECORD

My dog's first lesson was:_____

First trick:_____

Other tricks learned:_____

My dog attended _____ obedience class from _____

to_____. He graduated with a score of _____.

Other classes:

Date_____ Name of Class_____

Date_____ Name of Class_____

Date_____ Name of Class_____

Date_____ Name of Class_____

My Beardie can do the following:

Sit	Stay	Come	Down	Heel	Jump
Stand for Examination		Retrieve	Find an Object		Play Catch
Do Agility Exercises		Track	Search and Rescue		Play Flyball
Herd Ducks		Herd Sheep	Catch a Frisbee		Carry a Pack
Stack for Showing		Other:_____			

FAVORITE THINGS

Favorite Person:

Favorite Treat:

Favorite Food:

Favorite Toy:

Best Friend:

Likes to go:

Likes to play:

Likes to sleep (where):

1 *The Beardie Charisma*

The Bearded Collie is a "super dog" to those who love him. While not perfect for everyone, the breed is unique in its capabilities, endearing qualities, and timeless beauty. He is truly a gift from the past—with a heritage all but lost in many of today's breeds. The "Beardie" comes unchanged in beauty and spirit over the centuries. Today's breeder is faced with the awesome responsibility of preserving the virtues of the breed—virtues that are beyond price and that, once lost, can never be recovered.

The quotation in the front of this book depicts one aspect of the Beardie. A less romantic but more practical statement was made by Major James G. Logan of Scotland, a longtime Beardie fan:

> A Beardie is a dog of almost over-powering friendliness, extremely active, boisterous, an expert in escapology, a dog with a loud bark who is not afraid to use it. It is not a dog for the house proud or car proud or the fanatical gardener or for parents of nervous children or for those who are forced to leave it in the house all day, but for anyone who is prepared to train it and control it, to exercise it and to look after its coat, to put up with mud, sand or worse that it will bring into the house, and can keep it occupied, there is no breed which will provide more faithful companionship or greater entertainment.

There is no doubt that the more a Beardie is made a member of the family, worked with, talked to, and loved, the more personality he will develop.

Britannia Ride to Blue Heaven as she appeared on the front page of the Citizen in Prince George, Canada. Courtesy Velda Fitchett, D'Arbonne.

The Beardie charisma is a phenomenon not easily described. It has to do with the temperament and personality of each dog, but it is more than this. It is an interrelationship between person and dog that transcends mere ownership. It encompasses devotion, companionship—and perhaps most of all—a mutual respect. It instills in the person lucky enough to feel this bond a sense of responsibility to a particular animal.

TEMPERAMENT AND PERSONALITY

You have to live with a Beardie to appreciate his worth and character. Each individual is different from all others, yet all possess some traits that are uniquely Beardie—characteristics shared by others within the breed but that set Beardies apart from other breeds of dogs. Beardies are usually happy. They forgive easily and never hold grudges, yet they never miss a lesson along the way. Their enthusiasm for life and all that it offers can be contagious. They often make you laugh, not because they are intentionally clowning, but because they are just having fun, and they laugh with you. Beardies bubble over with love for everyone. They assume that everyone welcomes them with equal abandon, and a visitor may be surprised by a bear hug and kiss from the family Beardie.

Temperament is inherited. It dictates if a Beardie will be timid or aggressive, boisterous or quiet, responsive or stubborn. These basics cannot be changed drastically, and they will be passed on to offspring. Luckily, most Beardies are self-assured, steady, and sensible. To pick an individual that is anything less is to jeopardize your chance for a happy relationship with your dog. There is a wide range of acceptable temperaments, but neither a dog that is very timid nor one that is offensively aggressive should be considered "typical." Some Beardies are reserved with strangers and some are openly affectionate with everyone, but all must respond to their owners to be correct working dogs.

Temperament can be modified by the dog's environment. Proper socialization and training are beneficial, while abuse or neglect can create character flaws. Personality, on the other hand, is acquired by association with man. It is the full expression of individual characteristics developed within the limits of the dog's inherited temperament. Character, an important element in the Beardie charisma, is a combination of the dog's temperament and personality. A dog with sound character is one that behaves predictably and intelligently under any circumstances and that has enough personality to be an interesting companion.

When selecting a Beardie, choose one whose temperament appeals to you, as long as it falls within reasonable limits. One person might prefer a rambunctious animal, while another might select a sweet, quiet individual. The most important requisite at any age is responsiveness to the owner. This determines trainability, the ability to communicate, and the will to please.

Instinctive Behavior and Needs

In addition to temperament, any given individual inherits instinctive responses. In Beardies, the dominant instinct is to herd. This makes them extremely suitable as family dogs but also causes them to have certain requirements. Be aware that Beardies can be rather independent, and you as the owner must exert enough dominance to maintain control. Herding dogs have an inborn will to please yet a compulsion to complete a job with single-minded fanaticism. Beardies have been selected for centuries on the basis of intelligence balanced by responsiveness to people.

Beardies are also protective of their charges, which can include children, puppies, and other animals in place of a flock of sheep, and they may try to bunch their charges together. A Beardie is happiest if all members of his family are together, and if they are in separate rooms, he often will go back and forth between them. A mother dog will worry her puppies until she has them grouped together. The Beardie is not a guard dog, but he makes an outstanding nursemaid. It is believed that the original Nana in James Barrie's *Peter Pan* was a Bearded Collie. Do not expect him to attack an intruder; unless his people are actually threatened, such action would be contrary to a Beardie's nature.

Beardies are active and intelligent and are easily bored if neglected. Although they are well mannered and capable of amusing themselves, they crave a fair amount of personal contact and mental stimulation. A neglected Beardie may become unintentionally destructive. Beardies need owners who are consistent about training and who offer a firm but fair authority. Good parents usually make good Beardie owners.

House Dog or Kennel Dog?

Most Beardies make admirable house dogs. They like to keep their quarters clean and require little conscious housebreaking, and, of course, their personalities flourish best when they are part of the family. Although exuberant outdoors, they settle down and are well mannered after the initial greeting in the house.

Beardies do well under kennel conditions also, but they must be given adequate exercise and enough human contact for proper socialization. When you select a dog, be sure that he shows evidence of good socialization. A friendly, responsive Beardie will adjust well as a pet regardless of whether he has been raised in the house or in the kennel.

*Beardies are expert jumpers. Am. Can. Ch.
Bedlam's Go Get 'em Garth Can. Am. CD
in the air. Courtesy Alice Bixler.*

"eye" while working. History credits them with being herders but also records their service as drovers, working behind livestock being driven to market. Apparently Beardies excelled in both functions. This is remarkable, because most breeds specialize in only one of these tasks and must be taught the other chore against their instincts. Some modern herding books reference the Beardie as a drover, but this is not justified by the instinct tests that usually show the Beardie to be a herder. In fact, Beardies are one of the very few breeds capable of rivaling the Border Collie at its trials. Beardies have been able to command respect from Border Collie trainers who have seen them in action.

Documentation of the breed's history is incomplete, because Beardies belonged to the

A wildly exuberant, hesitant, or destructive dog is likely showing signs of neglect and will need individual attention before he behaves more favorably. He will probably adjust well with patience, but you will need to expend more effort than with a properly socialized puppy. It is far easier to get control of an extrovert than to give confidence to a timid dog.

A NEW START
FOR AN ANCIENT BREED

To appreciate the intricacies of the Beardie's nature, you must look to his heritage. Until very recent times, he has been strictly a working stock dog. Most Beardies exhibit herding characteristics similar to those of the Border Collie—they circle and bunch the flock, and some even display

*An acrobatic puppy shows off.
Courtesy Alice Bixler.*

hill shepherds rather than catching the nobleman's eye as a show breed. However, they are mentioned throughout several centuries and appear to be one of the oldest British breeds, tracing probably as far back as A.D. 1540 in recognizable form.

Records show that in about 1514, three Lowland Polish Sheepdogs—two bitches and a dog—were traded to a Scottish shepherd for a valuable ram and ewe. These individuals probably founded the breed that is known as the Bearded Collie. Some researchers believe that the breed was already established in Britain at the time of the Roman invasion. It is universally accepted that the Bearded Collie, like the Puli and most other shaggy sheepdog breeds, is descended from the Komondor of the Magyars in Central Europe

By the 1700s, Beardies were showing up regularly in British portraits and writings. Prior to 1900, the breed was often called the Highland Collie and was sometimes mentioned as the Hairy Moued [mouthed] Collie or the Mountain Collie. The word "collie" is derived from the Scottish term for any sheepdog, which is thought to be "coaley" [black] or the Welsh "coelio" [faithful].

By 1800, the breed was quite popular, and some individuals were even being bred for showing in southern Scotland. There were two distinct varieties. The Border or Lowland type was a large, slate-colored dog with long, harsh, straight hair. He often measured as tall as twenty-four or twenty-five inches at the shoulder. The brown-colored Highland variety was smaller and more agile. He had a shorter, curly coat. The two varieties were crossed to combine the best qualities of both in the modern Beardie. The curly coat has been bred out, and coat quality (either straight or slightly wavy) is now the same in all colors.

Although the Beardie was well established as a breed, no Standard or breed club existed until 1912. This led to the virtual extinction of the breed as a recognized entity. The breed was kept alive only by a few shepherds who raised Beardies to work sheep, and although the lineage was kept pure, there were no records or registrations. The Beardies were saved only because of their working ability and their resistance to the cold, rainy Scottish climate

Beardies are believed to figure prominently in the background of the more recent Border Collie and Old English Sheepdog breeds, and possibly the Kerry Blue Terrier. Indeed, a specimen with Beardie coat and characteristics still crops up now and then in registered Border Collie litters. The occasional smooth Beardie is an indication that the Border Collie could have been bred down from the Beardie with careful selection and perhaps a few outcrosses. Since Border Collies have always been selected for working ability rather than for type, it is likely that both rough and smooth varieties will be tolerated for some time in that breed. In Beardies, however, where the type has always been more uniform and distinctive, breeders chose to eliminate and not register the occasional smooth specimen. As a result, the smooth coats have virtually been eliminated.

Revival of the Show Beardie

In 1944 in England, Mrs. G.O. Williston accidently acquired a brown Beardie bitch puppy while searching for a working Shetland Sheepdog. It took her some time to realize that "Jeannie" was a Bearded Collie and not just a sheepdog cross, and by that time, Mrs. Williston had been thoroughly won over by the Beardie charm. From this bitch and from a few other Beardies of working lineage who became certified as purebred come all of the registered Beardies in the world today. Mrs. Williston engaged in a long and frustrating search for a suitable mate for Jeannie and eventually acquired a slate male whom she called Bailie of Bothkennar. The breed made a cautious comeback under her fostering. The Bearded Collie Club of Great Britain was formed in 1955, and in 1959 the breed gained championship status in England.

This is my kind of herding. Ch. Bedlam's Unreachable Star. Courtesy Alice Bixler.

Beardies quickly spread to other countries. The first litter whelped in the United States was bred by Mr. and Mrs. Lawrence Levy in 1967. The Bearded Collie Club of America (BCCA) was founded in 1969. The tireless efforts of a few early members resulted in the American Kennel Club (AKC) granting miscellaneous recognition to the breed in 1974 and entering the Bearded Collie in the AKC Stud Book with full working breed status in October 1976. Beardies began their show career in the United States on February 1, 1977, when the breed became eligible to compete in the Working Group. Their existence was made obvious to all when Ch. Brambledale Blue Bonnet CD won an all-breed Best in Show, a remarkable feat for any bitch, especially for one of a new, rare breed. Ch. Shiel's Mogador Silverleaf CD put the males in the record by taking a second Best in Show during the first year of recognition. Several other notable dogs won group placements, and a number of champions finished during 1977. The Bearded Collie established his reputation as a sound, stable working dog by show definition as well as by his proven herding ability. In January of 1983, the Working Group was divided, and the Beardie was put into the new Herding Group.

2 *Ideals and Interpretation*

An evaluation of any animal must involve comparing him to what he should be. In the show ring, the contender is judged against the other entrants. To the breeder, however, every individual must be compared to the ideal specimen of the breed. But what is ideal? Is this different for each person, or is there a common goal? Must the beginner be influenced by the opinion of only one established breeder? Where can you turn to find a *universal* concept of the perfect Beardie? The flawless Beardie does not exist, but the mental image of what he looks like is necessary for the breeder or fancier. It provides a goal toward which to strive with every selection and breeding.

Each recognized breed of dog has a written description of the "ideal" for that breed. This word picture is known as the Standard and is the final authority to which all breeders, judges, and students of the breed must turn. The Standard is often referred to as the blueprint for the breed; it allows for individual interpretation while drawing boundaries of acceptable variations

The original Standard was extremely vague and could actually have described a number of shaggy breeds. The AKC approved a revised Standard for the Bearded Collie in 1978. It was a great improvement over the original, but many members of the Bearded Collie Club of America feel that it still needs clarification, correction, and added details. Also, the AKC would like for all breed Standards to fit a uniform format. Any change in a Standard must be undertaken seriously, and the final product must be worthy of representing the breed for generations to come. Breeders must never presume to make the Standard fit the dogs; the dogs should always be bred to conform to a well-written Standard.

OFFICIAL AKC BEARDED COLLIE STANDARD

CHARACTERISTICS: The Bearded Collie is hardy and active, with an aura of strength and agility characteristic of a real working dog. Bred for centuries as a companion and servant of man, the Bearded Collie is a devoted and intelligent member of the family. He is stable and self-confident, showing no signs of shyness or aggression. This is a natural and unspoiled breed.

GENERAL APPEARANCE: The Bearded Collie is a medium-sized shaggy dog with a medium length coat that follows the natural lines of the body and allows plenty of daylight under the body. The body is long and lean, and, though strongly made, does not appear heavy. A bright, inquiring expression is a distinctive feature of the breed. The Bearded Collie should be shown in a natural stance.

HEAD: The head is in proportion to the size of the dog. The skull is broad and flat; the cheeks are well filled beneath the eyes; the muzzle is strong and full; the foreface is equal in length to the distance between the stop and occiput. The nose is large and squareish. A snipey muzzle is to be penalized. (See Color section for pigmentation.)'

Eyes: The eyes are large, expressive, soft and affectionate, but not round or protruding, and are set widely apart. The eyebrows are arched to the sides to frame the eyes and are long enough to blend smoothly into the coat on the sides of the head. (See Color section for eye color.)

Ears: The ears are medium sized, hanging, and covered with long hair. They are set level with the eyes. When the dog is alert, the ears have a slight lift at the base.

Teeth: The teeth are strong and white, meeting in a scissors bite. Full dentition is desirable.

NECK: The neck is in proportion to the length of the body, strong and slightly arched, blending smoothly into the shoulders.

FOREQUARTERS: The shoulders are well laid back at an angle of approximately forty-five degrees; a line drawn from the highest point of the shoulder blade to the forward point of articulation approximates a right angle with a line from the forward point of articulation to the point of elbow. The tops of the shoulder blades lie in against the withers, but they slope outwards from there sufficiently to accommodate the desired spring of ribs. The legs are straight and vertical with substantial, but not heavy, bone and are covered with shaggy hair all around. The pasterns are flexible without weakness.

BODY: The body is longer than it is high in an approximate ration of five to four, the length measured from point of chest to point of buttocks; the height measured at the highest point of the withers. The length of the back comes from the length of the ribcage

Eng. Ch. Pepperland Lyric John at Potterdale, Potterdale, a male of outstanding type.

Multi-group placing Ch. Lochengar Never Surrender exhibits femininity in a bitch.

and not that of the loin. The back is level. The ribs are well-sprung from the spine but are flat at the sides. The chest is deep, reaching at least to the elbows. The loins are strong. The level back line blends smoothly into the curve of the rump. A flat croup or a steep croup is to be severely penalized.

HINDQUARTERS: The hind legs are powerful and muscular at the thighs with well-bent stifles. The hocks are low. In normal stance the hocks are perpendicular to the ground and parallel to each other when viewed from the rear; the hind feet fall just behind a perpendicular line from the point of buttocks when viewed from the side. The legs are covered with shaggy hair all around.

Tail: The tail is set low and is long enough for the end of the bone to reach at least to the point of the hocks. It is normally carried low with an upward swirl at the tip while the dog is standing. When the dog is excited or in motion, the curve is accentuated and the tail may be raised but is never carried beyond a vertical line. The tail is covered with abundant hair.

FEET: The feet are oval in shape with the soles well padded. The toes are arched and close together, and well covered with hair including between the pads.

COAT: The coat is double with the undercoat soft, furry and close. The outer coat is flat, harsh, strong and shaggy, free from wooliness or curl, although a slight wave is permissible. The coat falls naturally to either side but must never be artificially parted. The length and density of the hair are sufficient to provide a protective coat and to enhance the shape of the dog, but not so profuse as to obscure the natural lines of the body. The dog should be shown as naturally as is consistent with good grooming, but the coat must not be trimmed in any way. On the head, the bridge of the nose is sparsely covered with hair which is slightly longer on the sides to cover the lips. From the cheeks, the lower lips and under the chin, the coat increases in length towards the chest, forming the typical beard. An excessively long, silky coat or one which has been trimmed in any way must be severely penalized.

COLOR: All Bearded Collies are born either black, blue, brown or fawn, with or without white markings. With maturity, the color may lighten, so that a born black may become any shade of gray from black to slate to silver, a born brown from chocolate to sandy. Blues and fawns also show shades from dark to light. Where white occurs, it only appears on the foreface as a blaze, on the skull, on the tip of the tail, on the chest, legs, and feet, and around the neck. The white hair does not grow on the body behind the shoulders nor on the face to surround the eyes. Tan markings occasionally appear and are acceptable on the eyebrows, inside the ears, on the cheeks, under the tail, and on the legs where white joins the main color.

Pigmentation: Pigmentation on the Bearded Collie follows the coat color. In a born black, the eye rims, nose, and lips are black, whereas in the born blue, the pigmentation is a blue-gray color. A born brown dog has brown pigmentation and born fawns a correspondingly lighter brown. The pigmentation is completely filled in and shows no sign of spots.

Eyes: Eye color will generally tone with the coat color. In a born blue or fawn, the distinctively lighter eyes are correct and must not be penalized.

SIZE: The ideal height at the withers is 21 to 22 inches for adult dogs and 20 to 21 inches for adult bitches. Height over and under the ideal is to be severely penalized. The express objective of this criterion is to insure that the Bearded Collie remains a medium-sized dog.

GAIT: Movement is free, supple and powerful. Balance combines good reach in forequarters with strong drive in hindquarters. The back remains firm and level. The feet are lifted only enough to clear the ground, giving the impression that the dog glides along making minimum contact. Movement is lithe and flexible to enable the dog to make the sharp turns and sudden stops required of the sheep dog. When viewed from the front or rear, the front and rear legs travel in the same plane from shoulder and hip joint to pads at all speeds. Legs remain straight, but feet move inward as speed increases until the edges of the feet converge on a center line at a fast trot.

SERIOUS FAULTS:
Snipey muzzle
Flat croup or steep croup
Excessively long, silky coat
Trimmed or sculptured coat
Height over or under the ideal

There are some prevalent discrepancies from the Standard to be seen in the show ring today. One of these is an increasing disregard for the insistence on naturalness. Dogs are seen with artificial parting down the back and obvious trimming, especially on the feet and legs, but also on necks, tails, belly lines, and faces. Much of this is done by professional handlers who think that it is necessary for Group and Best in Show competition. Other exhibitors, seeing a trimmed dog win, feel that they must do the same. If the dog is a good one and the owner tells the handler not to trim, the dog will still do his share of winning. It is permissible to do some judicious trimming of straggly areas that would be considered good grooming, but this should never be obvious or give a "sculpted" look.

Another area of divergence is the tendency toward shorter, broader dogs, rather than the long, lean look. These cobbier dogs are a move away from true working-dog type because they lack the endurance and agility necessary for a day's work. Their movement is somewhat more plodding rather than being free and supple. This tendency may be attributable to judges or breeders who have faulted Beardies for being too close in the rear. It stands to reason that a lean dog will have his hind legs closer together than a broad dog, but he can still have the correct straight line from hip to pad. Of course, if the dog is cow-hocked or crosses over, he should be penalized.

Several areas need to be addressed in any future changes in the Standard. One of these is the ear set. It would be better if the wording read, "The *orifice* of the ear is set level with the eyes." The current wording might encourage a houndlike ear. When a dog with correct ear set lifts his ears at the base, the lift should bring the ear about level with the top of the skull. This ability to lift the ear slightly is important, because it increases hearing capability and probably aids in ventilating the ear, thus avoiding problems such as ear infection. Hound ears lack the ability to lift.

The correct eye shape has been omitted in the Standard. A large, oval eye is preferred. Length of upper arm also is omitted. This should be equal in length to the shoulder blade. In the Standard, croups are described only in a negative manner. The correct slope for a Beardie should be about twenty-five degrees, which is slightly flatter than the thirty-degree slope common to most other working breeds. The Beardie developed this trait to be able to leap straight upward to facilitate his sheep herding on the rough Scottish countryside. The flatter croup and corre-

Lovely head type. Eng. Ch. Bravo of Bothkennar, Osmart.

Parcana Possibility, Silverleaf, shows correct coat texture.

spondingly squared-off topline are distinctive breed characteristics.

Recent studies indicate that a well-laid-back shoulder may actually measure less than the accepted forty-five degree angle. Dogs with ideal layback that were previously assumed to have a forty-five degree shoulder angulation probably measure closer to thirty-nine degrees. This discrepancy is due strictly to methods of measurement and is not intended to advocate straighter shoulder angulation.

Some minor comments concerning the color section are in order. First is the color of the pigmentation of fawns. While fawn could be considered just a lighter shade of brown, it actually has a distinctly mauve tone. This is the surest way to distinguish between a true fawn and a light brown. Two other areas are more a matter of interpretation than a need for change. The phrase, "The white does not grow on the face to surround the eyes," should never, by any stretch of the imagination, be interpreted to fault a blaze that arches over the eyes as the hair lengthens. The unacceptable white is seen as a predominantly white head or a blaze so wide that it encompasses the eyes at the skin line.

The reference that pigmentation should have no spots means that no flesh-colored spots should appear on the nose leather, the visible part of the lips, or the eye rims. It does not refer to a pink spot on the bridge of the muzzle---a normal occurrence in any breed that has white markings on the face.

A most desirable change in the Standard would be to eliminate the list of Serious Faults and to substitute the statement, "The foregoing

Bites: left, correct scissors bite; right, overshot bite — incorrect for an adult, but may correct if seen in a puppy.

Bottom left: correct ear set. Bottom right: ears set too high.

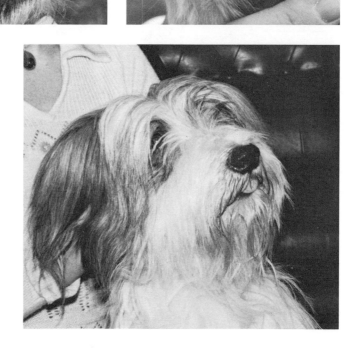

PARTS OF THE BEARDIE

1. Foreface or muzzle. Well filled below the eyes. Broad and blunt.
2. Stop. Nose to stop should be equal to or slightly shorter in length than stop to occiput. Stop should be well defined.
3. Occiput.
4. Line indicating center of gravity.
5. Withers. The point to which height is measured.
6. Back. Moderately long, strong, and level.
7. Loin. Close coupled and muscular. Loin is the area between last rib and hipbone.
8. Croup. Should have slight downward slope.
9. Tail. Must reach at least to the hock. Low carriage is preferred.
10. Thigh. Well muscled and long.
11. Hock. Low set and flexible.
12. Stifle. Should be long and well bent.
13. Flank. Slightly tucked up.
14. Elbow. Depth of chest should reach at least to this point.
15. Pastern. Should be strong and moderately sloped.
16. Upper arm. Angle of upper arm is measured where a line from point of shoulder to point of elbow intersects the perpendicular.
17. Point of shoulder.
18. Throatlatch.
19. Underjaw. Should be of sufficient length to provide for correct bite and allow lips to meet evenly.
20. Nose. Should be large and square.
21. Length of body measured from point of shoulder to point of hip. Standard calls for five-to-four ratio of length to height. Much of this length is due to proper angulation and length of rib cage.

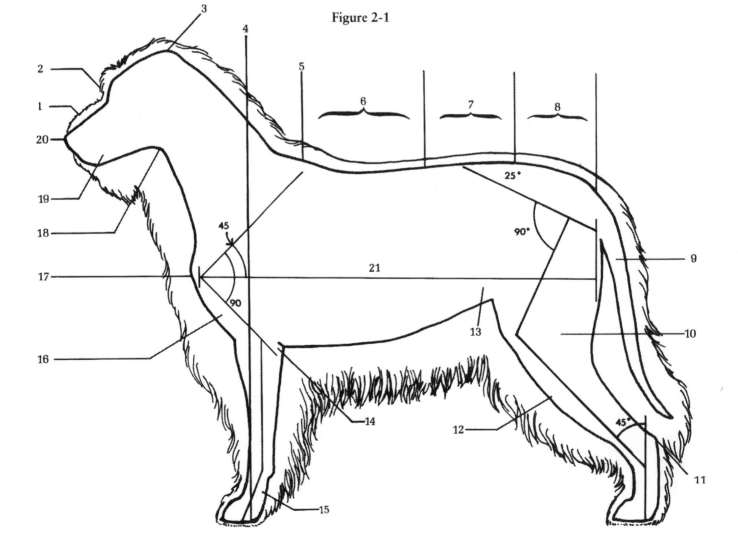

Figure 2-1

STRUCTURE OF THE BEARDIE

1. Skull. Should be broad and flat.
2. Neck. Moderately long and arched.
3. Rib cage. Long, sloping well back, with moderate spring flattened at the bottom.
4. Thoracic vertebrae.
5. Lumbar vertebrae.
6. Croup (sacrum).
7. Pelvis (ilium).
8. Pelvis (ischium).
9. Upper thigh (femur). "Rear angulation" refers to the angle at which the upper thigh meets the pelvis.f The ideal is ninety degrees.
10. Stifle joint (patella).
11. Stifle (tibia and fibula). Should be equal to or preferably longer than the thigh bone.
12. Hock joint.
13. Metatarsus.
14. Elbow (olecranon).
15. Feet (phalanges).
16. Pastern (metacarpus).
17. Pastern joint.
18. Forearm (radius and ulna).
19. Upper arm (humerus). Should be equal in length to the shoulder blade. Actual length of bone is measured rather than to point of elbow.
20. Breastbone (prosternum). Projects slightly in front of point of shoulder, but should not be prominent.
21. Shoulder blade (scapula). "Front angulation" refers to the angle at which the scapula and humerus meet. Ideal angle is ninety degrees. Shoulder blade should be set at a forty-five-degree angle.
22. Cheekbones. Should be flat and merge smoothly with the skull without dips or ridges.

Figure 2-2

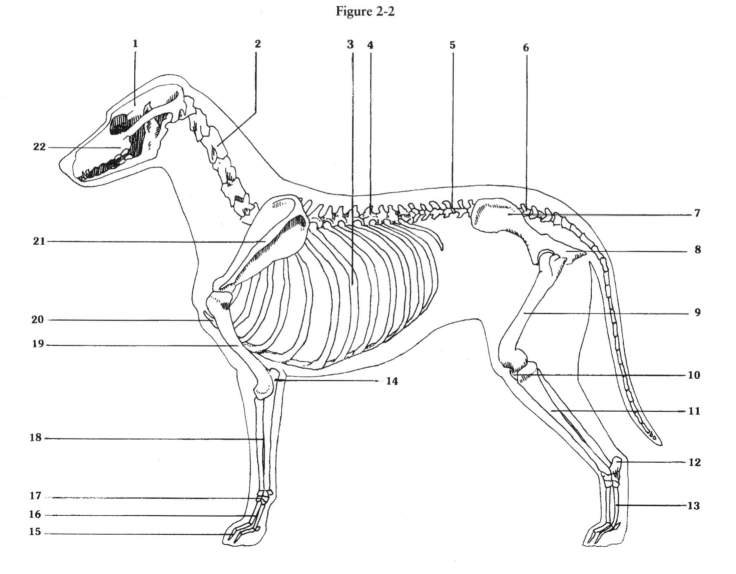

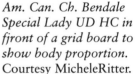

Am. Can. Ch. Bendale Special Lady UD HC in fjront of a grid board to show body proportion. Courtesy MicheleRitter.

is a description of the ideal Bearded Collie, any deviation to be penalized according to the extent of the deviation."

On the whole, this Standard is a tribute to those who compiled it. It is to be hoped that any changes will be as carefully thought out. It is interesting to compare the BCCA Standard with that of the Bearded Collie Club in England.

BRITISH STANDARD

GENERAL APPEARANCE: Lean, active dog, longer than it is high in an approximate ratio of five to four, measured from point of chest to point of buttock. Bitches may be slightly longer. Though strongly made, should show plenty of daylight under body and should not look too heavy. Bright, enquiring expression is a distinctive feature.

CHARACTERISTICS: Alert, lively, self-confident and active.

TEMPERAMENT: Steady, intelligent working dog, with no signs of nervousness or aggression

HEAD AND SKULL: Head in proportion to size. Skull broad, flat and square, distance between stop and occiput being equal to width between orifices of ears. Muzzle strong and equal in length to distance between stop and occiput. Whole effect being that of a dog with strength of muzzle and plenty of brain room. Moderate stop. Nose large and square, generally black but normally following coat colour in blues and browns. Nose and lips of solid colour without spots or patches. Pigmentation of lips and eye rims follows nose colour.

EYES: Toning with coat colour, set widely apart and large, soft and affectionate, not protruding. Eyebrows arched up and forward but not so long as to obscure eyes.

EARS: Of medium size and drooping. When alert, ears lift at base, level with, but not above top of skull, increasing apparent breadth of skull.

MOUTH: Teeth large and white. Jaws strong with a perfect, regular and complete scissors bite preferred, i.e., upper teeth closely overlapping lower teeth and set square to the jaws. Level bite tolerated but undesirable.

NECK: Moderate length, muscular and slightly arched.

FOREQUARTERS: Shoulders sloping well back. Legs straight and vertical with good bone, covered with shaggy hair all round. Pasterns flexible without weakness.

BODY: Length of back comes from length of rib cage and not that of the loin. Back level and ribs well sprung but not barrelled. Loin strong and chest deep, giving plenty of heart and lung room.

HINDQUARTERS: Well muscled with good second thighs, well- bent stifles and low hocks. Lower leg falls at right angle to ground and, in normal stance, is just behind a line vertically below point of buttocks.

FEET: Oval in shape with soles well padded. Toes arched and close together, well covered with hair, including between pads.

TAIL: Set low, without kink or twist, and long enough for end of bone to reach at least point of hock. Carried low with an upward swirl at tip whilst standing or walking, may be extended at speed. Never carried over back. Covered with abundant hair.

GAIT/MOVEMENT: Supple, smooth and long reaching, covering ground with minimum effort

COAT: Double with soft, furry and close undercoat. Outer coat flat, harsh, strong and shaggy, free from wooliness and curl, though slight wave permissible. Length and density of hair sufficient to provide a protective coat and to enhance shape of dog, but not enough to obscure natural lines of body. Coat must not be trimmed in any way. Bridge of nose sparsely covered with hair slightly longer on side to cover lips. From cheeks, lower lips and under chin, coat increases in length towards chest, forming typical beard.

COLOUR: Slate grey, reddish fawn, black, blue, all shades of grey, brown and sandy with or without white markings. When white occurs it appears on foreface, as a blaze on skull, on tip of tail, on chest,

legs and feet and, if round the collar, roots of white hair should not extend behind shoulder. White should not appear above hocks on outside of hind legs. Slight tan markings are acceptable on eyebrows, inside ears, on cheeks, under root of tail and on legs where white joins the main colour.

SIZE: Ideal height: Dogs 53 to 56 centimeters (21 to 22 inches); bitches 51 to 53 centimeters (20 to 21 inches). Overall quality and proportions should be considered before size but excessive variations from the ideal height should be discouraged.

FAULTS: Any departure from the foregoing points should be considered a fault and the seriousness with which the fault should be regarded should be in exact proportion to its degree.

NOTE: Male animals should have two apparently normal testicles fully descended into the scrotum.

A comparison of the two Standards shows far more similarities than differences. The English Standard more precisely defines the amount of white allowed on the hind legs, the size of the skull, and the ear placement. The American Standard gives more detail on the rib shape and a far better description of gait. The English ask for eyebrows to arch upward and forward, while the Americans say to the sides, although this is probably as much a matter of grooming as genetics. The English have a much better section on Faults. It covers all bases and puts all faults in proportion. The American Standard gives the erroneous impression that faults not listed are not really serious. It would be absurd to think that a trimmed coat, which is non-hereditary, could be more serious than a structural fault, which is not only genetic but could be incapacitating. It is to be hoped that any future change in the American Standard would adopt the English version. Many other breed Standards use this wording.

Ch. Parcana Jake McTavish in top form!

Ch. Parcana Lord Corwin CD HC BIS.
© Debrah Helen Muska, Animal Images.

Left: Am. Can. Ch. Britannia Ticket To Ride HC ROMX;
Right: Ch. Britannia Sweet Lady CD.

Am. Can. Ch. Bendale Special Lady UD HC.

Am.Can. Ch. Britannia Just Jeffrey HC and his daughter, Am. Can. Ch. Britannia Sweet Libeardie.

Ch. Bedlam's Nemesis in New York's Central Park.

Bridgrove Black Rory.

Above: Am. Can. Ch. Britannia Ticket to Ride HC ROMX winning BOB at Westminster Kennel Club, 1993. Owner handled by Michele Ritter. He went on to a Group Second.

Right: Ch. Daybreak Rising Sun UD, CD. Breeeder/owner Barbara Prescott.

Ch. Aretisan Bronze Paladin HS.

Flyball is an exciting sport enjoyed by Alice Bixler's Beardie.

Ch. Highlander Double Enchanted HC, owned by Don and Elodji Means and Beth Tilson.

Britannia Master Thinker UD, HI, Can. CD, sporting his herding ribbons. Owned by Sandy Weiss.

Ch. Highlander Spellbound HC, ROM, CGC retrieving in the water.

Beth Tilson with three lovely veterans (left to right): Ch. Highlander Lorna Doone CD, HC, ROM, ROM I at age seven years; Ch. Parchment Farm's Mr. Kite CD HC ROM, at ten years; and Parchment Farm's Annie Laurie HC at eleven years.

Five-week-old brown, fawn, and black puppies.

A rainbow of colors in one litter. Left to right: brown, blue, black, fawn, brown, and tricolor.

A black Beardie: Am. Can. Ch. Crisch Midnight Magic, HC ROM. Graham Photo.

A fawn puppy:
Parcana Sir Raggs of Genesee.

A lighter fawn adult: Ch. Britannia Fawn Lady.
Photo by Jezierski.

A rare black and tan Beardie, Ch. Higllandglen
Gruff McDuff. This color was written out of the
British Standard in the 1960s.

Four colors of Beardies:
Left to right, a black, a fawn, a brown, and a gray.

A slate: Ch. Madigan's Born for Adventure.

A brown Am. Ch. Willowmead Red Ruariridh.

Fawns: Ch. Stonehaven's My Lady Amber, left, and her dam, Ch. Stonehaven's Picture Perfect.

3 Moving Out

A Beardie's effectiveness as a working dog is primarily determined by his physical ability. He must be swift, tireless, and capable of sudden starts, stops, and turns. He also has developed the unique ability to leap straight upward from any position, a feat that is useful in coping with the rough terrain and the half-wild sheep found in the Beardie's native habitat.

While some aspects of structure influence efficiency of movement more than others, a dog's conformation can be evaluated quickly and relatively accurately by watching how he moves. Show-ring evaluation of movement is made from three angles—as the dog approaches the judge, as he gaits away from the judge, and from the side as he circles the ring. Equal emphasis should be placed on each segment of gait. A dog that moves correctly is said to be "sound." (This term can also refer to proper health and temperament but usually is applied to gait.)

When evaluating soundness, a judge looks for straightness and strength of legs, ligamentation of joints, and musculature. These traits determine how well a dog will move within the limitations of his skeletal structure. Evaluation is also made on strength of topline and smoothness of motion, on where the feet hit the ground, and on the balance of the trot as determined by skeletal proportions and angles. If everything is correct, the Beardie will exhibit a long, easy, effortless stride that he can continue to use mile after mile. Conditioning the muscles will enable a dog to exhibit his greatest potential (*see* Chapter 7).

The natural working-dog gait is the trot. Because this is also the gait at which structure can most easily be evaluated, it is the only gait used in the show ring. The trot is achieved when the diagonal legs move in unison. It is a two-beat gait, with periods of suspension between each beat in which all four legs are off the ground at once. Length of stride is determined by the dog's "angulation." Front angulation is measured at the point of the shoulder; ideally, ninety degrees between the shoulder blade and the upper arm, which should be of equal length for maximum efficiency. Rear angulation is measured at the junction of the hip and thighbone—also a ninety-degree measurement in the ideal specimen. The thigh should be relatively long to allow for strong drive. In order for the trot to remain balanced, front and rear angulation must be the same. Therefore, if the ideal is not available, it is preferable to have a dog with a balanced front and rear angulation even though the angle is not perfect, rather than an individual that is well angulated at one end but poorly so at the other. The unbalanced dog cannot trot properly and must compensate in some aspect of his movement. Any gait deviation creates a weak point that, under prolonged stress or old age, is subject to breakdown.

SIDE GAIT

The speed and endurance of a dog is determined by his side gait. To many breeders, this is the most important aspect of gait, because it has the greatest effect on the dog's efficiency. Unfortunately, it is also the most difficult for a beginner to recognize. It is imperative that any serious Beardie enthusiast learn to analyze side gait.

The correct trot viewed from the side is effortless and powerful. The feet should be lifted only enough to clear the ground with a minimum of wasted vertical motion. This gives a Beardie the appearance of almost floating across the terrain. A bounce or roll to the topline is evidence of improper action. The topline should remain firm and level at all times

The hindquarters provide the forward propulsion known as "drive." The front should move in line with and at the same efficiency as the rear in order to accept the drive and provide the primary balance and directional control. The front action is referred to as "reach."

The right hind leg and the left front leg move together, and the left hind leg and right foreleg move in unison. One set of diagonals hits the ground, completes the stride, and lifts for a period of suspension; then the second set of diagonals strikes the ground and propels the dog forward before another moment of suspension. Then the process repeats. As one set of diagonals is projecting the dog forward, the other is clearing the ground and stretching forward to start the next stride. The hind foot will usually strike the ground at the point where the front foot on the same side just left. Legs on the same side come together under the body in a "V", then extend fully to the front and rear as the legs on the other side come together. To rec-

Figure 3-1
The correct trot. At full extension, all four feet are off the ground.

ognize a correct trot, watch for the diagonals moving in unison and for good length of stride.

Breaking down the trot even further, let's examine the front alone. The shoulder layback, the length and angle of the upper arm, and the leg and pastern all contribute to proper reach. The feet must be strong and resilient to absorb the shock. The front leg reaches as far forward as possible (in a good mover it should extend as far forward as the tip of the nose or slightly farther) and strikes the ground in unison with the hind diagonal. It then carries the dog forward until the front foot is underneath the body as far as possible, lifts just enough to clear the ground, and again reaches forward to accept the next stride. The hind foot follows a similar pattern. It reaches underneath the body and pushes the dog forward. Once it passes the vertical, it begins the portion of the stride known as follow-through, which provides much of the forward push. The foot should remain on the ground until both stifle and hock joints are at full extension, then lift only enough to clear the ground as it again moves forward.

Croup, thigh, stifle, hock, and foot, plus muscling, all contribute to proper rear action. The Beardie has a slightly flatter croup than most working breeds. This allows for an extended follow-through in drive, and, combined with the strong muscles and lighter frame, permits the freedom for flat-footed leaps. When all of this is put together, you see a graceful, startlingly agile dog in action. The longer and better balanced a trot, the longer and more effortlessly a dog can function

Faults of Side Gait

Unbalanced Stride. The least severe side fault is one in which the dog is balanced but poorly angulated and must take more steps to keep up. With this fault, timing and cadence are still correct. More severe side faults are usually due to incorrect skeletal proportions. The cause of these faults can vary from unbalanced angulation to disproportionate length of individual bones

A dog that has good rear angulation but inadequate shoulder layback is an all-too-common sight in many breeds, including Beardies. Although a dog with this fault has good drive, the front cannot keep up. The dog loses cadence in his trot and throws his front feet in an

Figure 3-2
*Maximum reach is limited
by shoulder angulation.*

Figure 3-3
Front feet lifted too high due to straight shoulders.

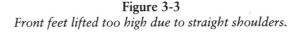

Figure 3-4
Downhill runner.

Figure 3-5
Kicking up.

Figure 3-6
Pounding or dwelling.

attempt to keep them away from his hind feet. Usually the front feet are lifted too high in a jerky motion. In a severe case, the hind feet strike the front legs and the dogs looks as if he is trying to kick his chin. The shoulder is fairly rigid and lacks flexibility. Some individuals take short, picky steps and lift the rear feet very high in order to expend the extra drive. In any case, the back does not remain level, but instead bounces when the animal is in motion.

Likewise, a dog that is better in shoulder than in stifle angulation has problems. Probably he will appear to be running downhill when on the level, because as he moves, his rear remains higher than his withers. A dog that is straight in rear angulation usually has a kick-up, or at least inadequate follow-through. His hind foot never reaches the print left by the front foot. Because the stride is shorter, power of the drive is reduced severely. Again, timing is thrown off and efficiency is below par.

When synchronization of gait is disturbed, a dog may exhibit "pounding" or "dwelling." The front foot reaches full extension, hesitates in midair, then crashes down after the hind leg has begun the next stride. This is extremely hard on the entire front assembly. It may be difficult to detect at first; watch for the diagonals moving together as an indication of correct gait.

Another indication is to look for the two inverted "V"s made when the legs are at full extension. The front and rear "V" should be equal in width, should not overlap, and should be simultaneous. A narrower front "V" denotes lack of reach, a narrower rear "V" a lack of drive. If they overlap, the dog is too short in body and probably crabs. If the "V"s are not simultaneous, the timing of the trot is off.¡

Hocks Set Too High. This is an imperfection that often (but not always) accompanies straight stifles. When both faults appear, the dog usually is high in the rear. The hind legs lack flexibility and the stride is shortened. Kick-up sometimes occurs and is quite noticeable in a dog with high hocks.

Sickle Hocks. This is a condition in which the metatarsus curves slightly inward from hock to foot. Follow-through becomes virtually impossible, and a stiff, stilted rear action results. Kick-up always occurs with sickle hocks. This condition is more common in Beardies than in many working breeds and should be faulted severely.

Short Upper Arm or Stifle. The upper arm should be equal in length to the shoulder blade. Regardless of angulation, a short upper arm throws off gait. (Upper-arm length is measured by the actual length of the bone, not to the point of elbow.) A hackney or prancing gait, with the front feet lifted high, is often indicative of a short upper arm. Less common is the proportionally shorter stifle. This results in a choppy rear action, which again lacks in follow-through.

Incorrect Pastern. The pastern is designed to absorb shock from the forequarters. It needs

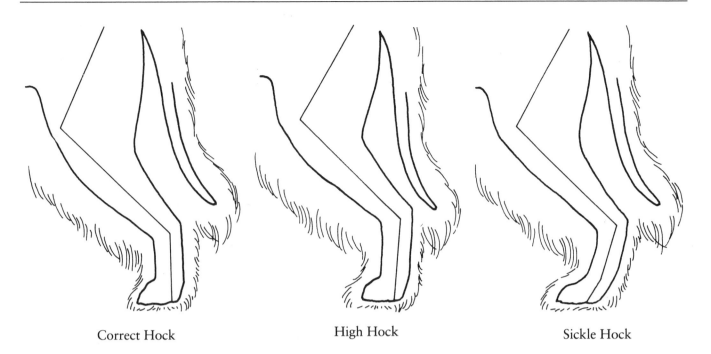

Correct Hock High Hock Sickle Hock

Figure 3-7
Correct and faulty hocks.

to be moderate in length and slope to perform its function efficiently. Too much slope results in loose, extremely weak wrists, a problem often accompanied by a crooked front. The other extreme is a too-steep pastern, which usually is short and often occurs in conjunction with a straight shoulder. Either condition is restrictive, and jarring strains the entire front assembly. The pastern is primarily a shock absorber, and under stress, a front assembly with poor pasterns will become sore and break down.

Pacing. Pacing is an action similar to trotting but one in which the legs on the same side (instead of the diagonals) move in unison. Sometimes a dog will pace quite rapidly. Unless the handler is aware of the difference in gait, a dog might pace in the show ring. Because structural analysis cannot be made from a pace, an individual that fails to trot readily will not be considered in a conformation class. The dog will often pace if the handler moves too slowly or if the dog is tired. A quick jerk will usually put the animal into a trot.

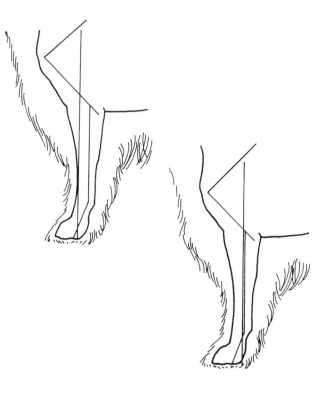

Figure 3-8
Length of upper arm.
Right: Short upper arm, causing foreleg to be set too far forward.

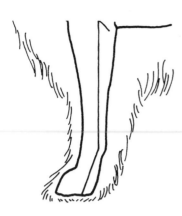

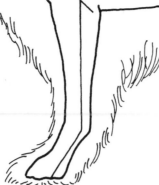

Correct   Long and Weak   Too Short

Figure 3-9
Pasterns.

Crabbing. Crabbing is the lack of alignment of the body in motion. The dog moves somewhat sideways, with the rear tracking to the left or right of the front. This last consideration of side gait is more easily seen coming or going. In some instances, crabbing is a way for the dog to avoid striking his front legs with his hind feet—the result of too short a body or of having more angulation in the rear than in the front. Crabbing may also be simply a bad habit.

Crabbing.

REAR OR "GOING" GAIT

The primary function of the dog's rear legs is to produce the drive that propels the body forward. However, the Standard also calls for the stance to be square and the gait true going away. It is certainly more pleasing to the eye this way and also avoids encouraging weaknesses that may break down under stress. A dog with a less-than-perfect stance but that moves well is superior to an individual that stands correctly but cannot move properly. Stance can always be trained or "stacked," but movement is proof of structure.

To determine how well a dog is tracking in rear, draw an imaginary line down the center of each hind leg (as viewed from the rear), from hip to hock to foot. When the dog is standing, these lines should be straight, vertical, and parallel to each other. A deviation at the hock or foot, either in or out, indicates a weakness. When the animal is moving, these lines should remain straight but come together in a "V" shape as speed increases. The inside edges of the feet converge on a center line; thus the term "singletrack" describing correct gait in a Beardie. Beardies sometimes appear a bit narrow because of their long stifles and leaner builds. Also, the long coat can be deceptive. Brush hocks thoroughly, or better yet, wet them down, before evaluating rear action.

Far left: Correct rear stance.

Figure 3-10
Left: Singletrack viewed from the rear.

Figure 3-11
Below: Pawprints made when a Beardie singletracks. Dark and light prints represent opposing diagonals.

Rear Faults

Hocking Out. Hocking out is probably the most serious of the rear faults because it puts terrific stress on the ligaments and is likely to restrict the drive of the hindquarters. The condition is permissible in young puppies because it is likely to be caused by loose ligamentation that will tighten as the dog grows. Very slight hocking out is like any other fault—the severity is judged by its degree rather than by its nature.

Cow Hocks, Toeing Out, and Close Rears. The term "cow hocks" is used when the hocks turn inward and the feet turn outward. If the legs are straight at the hocks but the feet turn outward, the dog is said to "toe out." True cow hocks exhibit both problems.

Among the first faults that a novice learns to recognize are light eyes, wavy coats, gay tails, and cow hocks. Because cow hocks are eventually determined to be the most serious of these faults, the novice will think of them as

Figure 3-12
Hocking out.

Figure 3-13
Cow hocks.

Figure 3-14
Toeing out.

Figure 3-15
Close parallel rear.

Figure 3-16
Crossing over.

Figure 3-17
Wide parallel rear.

paramount among structural faults. But the truth is that there are many worse and harder-to-detect faults than cow hocks. Cow hocks do not affect the rest of the dog unless they are so extreme as to constitute an actual deformity. A dog may appear cow hocked standing but still move true. This is a lesser fault than moving cow hocked.

To a lesser degree than cow hocks, toeing out and close rears are undesirable. In the latter two cases, the efficiency of gait is not badly restricted. Toeing out sometimes affects stance only, whereas a close parallel rear is also obvious in motion. A close parallel rear is one that, in motion, is parallel from hock to foot with an angle at the hock. This condition is often accompanied by a narrow pelvis.

Crossing Over. Crossing over is a a fault in which the feet overstep the center line and cross to the opposite side. The legs actually cross when gaiting, and the entire rear of the dog usually bounces from side to side as the center of gravity is shifted with each step. The fault becomes more obvious with speed.

The Wide Parallel Rear. A Beardie with this fault often (though not necessarily) stands perfectly; in fact, he is often touted as not being able to stand incorrectly. He is built like a table with unyielding vertical legs that remain the same distance apart at the feet in a swift trot as when standing. The wide parallel gait is more obvious at a slow gait, because the fast trot forces the legs toward a singletrack for balance. Wide rears are seldom seen in Beardies, and when this fault does occur, it is usually accompanied by a short or straight stifle. Occasionally, a wide mover, particularly one that is wide both front and rear, develops a characteristic "roll" from throwing his weight from side to side. This dog varies from the individual that hocks out in that the hocks of a wide mover remain in line and appear strong. Wide rear rarely affects side gait.

Hitching. Hitching occurs when one hind leg is lifted higher than the other as it is brought forward. This can be observed from the side as well and causes an imbalance in the gait. This possibly results from a difference in the amount of muscle in the legs and is rarely structural.

FRONT OR "COMING" GAIT

Beardies should also singletrack in front at a brisk trot. When the dog stands, his legs should be in straight parallel lines from elbows to pasterns to feet.

Correct front action is partially dependent on correct rib spring. Proper ribs are rounded at the top half to allow plenty of room for the heart and lungs but are flattened on the bottom half to allow for unrestricted swing of the front leg backward along the side of the dog. If the sides are too rounded (barrel-ribbed) or too flat (slab-sided), the plane in which the elbow moves is distorted and some of the efficiency in gait is destroyed. Barrel ribs often lack depth, and their roundness causes the elbows to swing out to avoid interference. A slab-sided individual lacks substance and appears frail and narrow. Although a normal condition in a young dog, slab-sidedness usually causes a faulty front action because the front is not adequately supported. Be wary of the young dog that is extremely well-developed in ribs and chest for his age because he may very well continue to develop and end up being too broad and heavy in front.

Front Faults

Crooked Front Legs. Crooked front legs are somewhat comparable to cow hocks in the rear. The legs bow outward at the top, inward at the pasterns, then out again at the foot. A dog with a crooked front may move well, but he often possesses other front faults that complicate the issue. Carried to the extreme, this front is known as "fiddle front." Beardies with narrow, crooked fronts should not be bred.

Out at Elbows. This fault is similar to hocking out. The elbows project out from the body rather than moving straight back and forth when the dog trots. This action can also be caused by excessive weight but is often a result of barrel ribs. Elbowing out is often found in conjunction with crooked legs, toeing in, a short upper arm, or loose ligamentation.

Wide Front. This fault means that the dog does not move in a singletrack. The dog usually stands nicely, but his legs remain vertical and parallel when in motion. This condition is similar to a wide parallel rear and can be caused by barrel ribs.

Figure 3-18
Singletrack viewed from the front.

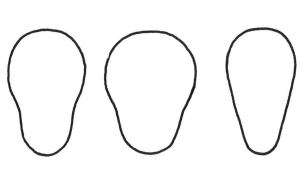

Figure 3-19
Ribspring.
Correct, barrel, and slab-sided.

Figure 3-20
Crooked front.

Figure 3-21
Out at elbows.

Figure 3-22
Wide front.

Figure 3-23
Narrow front.

Figure 3-24
Paddling.

Figure 3-25
Winging.

Figure 3-26
Crossing over.

Narrow or "Tied-In" Front. This refers to a dog that is narrow-chested and too close or pinched at the elbows. The legs may or may not be straight, but they lack adequate support from the rib cage and chest. As a result, the front exhibits an eggbeater motion or is thrown randomly from side to side. This type of front in a young dog may improve as the chest broadens with maturity provided the legs are straight. However, the feet often point outward. An individual that exhibits this fault should be considered a very questionable risk, even as a youngster.

Paddling. Paddling occurs when the dog throws his leg in an outward circle from the elbow as he moves. A dog that paddles usually tracks wide.

Ch. Sunkap Sir Knight HT at seven months of age showing proper front and rear extension and correct balance of stride.

Winging. Winging is often erroneously called "paddling." While both faults involve throwing the feet outward, winging originates at the pastern rather than at the elbow. Winging is seen more frequently than true paddling.

Crossing Over. Crossing over is the same fault as crossing in the rear. The feet pass beyond the center line, and the center of gravity shifts, causing a choppy, bouncing appearance. Crossing in front is usually due to a narrow chest.

Poor fronts have long been a problem in all breeds and are particularly noticeable in a sound working breed such as the Beardie. Once lost from a line, correct front structure is difficult to regain, but once obtained, it can be bred consistently with little effort. Breeding for good fronts should be a high priority in the breed.

Anything that interferes with the desired smooth-floating trot is faulty. The problems described above are examples, but they do not cover every possibility for faults. The complex interrelationship between parts of the body can easily be disturbed, so it is imperative to breed only individuals that are correct in structure.

"Bonnie and friend," courtesy of Melita Bearded Collies. Photo by Bill McKnown.

4 *Love at First Sight*

Almost everyone loves to shop—especially when the object of their search is a cuddly, lovable puppy. Before you get all wrapped up in the excitement of buying, make some practical deliberations. Your new Beardie will probably be a member of your household for a decade or more, and his selection deserves careful consideration.

As a potential dog owner, you may not have given any real thought to what type of dog will fit your needs. You may be attracted to a particular breed, such as the Beardie, because a friend has one or because you have seen pictures of the breed. However, you may not have stopped to assess the suitability of the breed to your family or situation. Before you embark on a dog-shopping spree, take time to research a number of breeds. Learn about their temperaments, care and space requirements, size, and hereditary strengths and weaknesses. Excellent sources for this information include books, veterinarians, the local kennel club breeder-referral or rescue service, and, of course, breeders themselves.

Will the breed that you admire fit in with your home? Consider your lifestyle, the age of your children, and your own temperament, as well as your space limitations. What will your dog be—a family pet, the foundation for a kennel, a working dog, an obedience dog for competition or a 4-H project, a show dog, or a combination of these? Where will you keep him? Do you have the time and money to provide him with proper care and attention?

Do not start looking for a Beardie until you are sure that this is the breed for you and that you are willing and able to make him a true member of your family. He will need your companionship and a reasonable amount of training. He will also need regular grooming. A Beardie is not a dog that you can leave alone in the backyard for weeks and then suddenly decide to bring in the house for a while. If this is your idea of the way to have a pet, you better look for another breed because you would not be happy with a Beardie.

SOME OBVIOUS QUESTIONS

Once you have decided on a Beardie, three additional questions are of major importance and should be considered before you shop. They are: what sex, what age, and what quality of dog do you need?

He, She, or It?

There are many old wives' tales about which makes a better pet—a male or female? Basically, it is a matter of personal preference, because either sex makes a marvelous pet. Beardies show more differences between individual puppies than between sexes. Rather than consider only one sex, it is better to look for the temperament that would best fit your lifestyle. This could be found in either a male or female puppy. A responsible breeder will be able to help you determine which puppy will best fill your needs. Once a pet is neutered, there is even less difference in the sexes.

Most reputable breeders require the neutering of a pet-quality Beardie when he is old enough. Neutering benefits both you *and* the breed by preventing unwanted litters and the perpetuation of mediocre-quality Beardies. It also eliminates the bothersome heat periods in a female or the tendency for a male to wander and fight. A neutered Beardie will be a more affectionate pet and a better worker, less prone to being distracted, and he will be easier to manage. There are health benefits as well, primarily reduced risk of mammary-gland or testicular cancer.

Neutering is safe, easy, and relatively inexpensive. Sluggishness, unwanted weight gain, temperament change, or other side effects rarely

Who can resist the adorable face of a Beardie puppy? Bedlam's Photogenic. Courtesy Alice Bixler.

occur provided the neutering is performed when the dog is old enough to have an adequate supply of sex hormones (approximately eight months of age). *Nothing* is gained by allowing your male to sire puppies or your bitch to whelp a litter before having him or her neutered. In fact, either could have negative effects.

Of course, if you want to breed or show, a neutered dog is not for you. Neutered animals or ones with a nonbreeding registry cannot be shown in conformation classes at any licensed show, but they can be shown in obedience or herding events.

The foundation for a breeding kennel should be the best bitch that you can find (*see* Chapter 11). It is usually not advisable to start

Seven-week-old Beardie puppies bred by Pat McDonald.

with a male, because the best males in the country are readily available for your use. Never start a breeding kennel with a male/female pair. Even if you are lucky enough to find suitable mates, they may not produce well together, and if perchance they do, you will still have to go outside to continue your program after the first couple of litters.

Males are impressive and are apt to become top show winners; therefore, some exhibitors prefer to start with a male. Even if you do not plan to breed, a top winning male can be promoted at stud if you can take the time and provide the facilities to handle visiting bitches.

Toddler, Teenager, or Adult?

Generally, you will think of getting a puppy at weaning age—seven to nine weeks—but there are many good reasons to buy an older Beardie. If you have very young children, a twelve-week-old puppy may better contend with their rough handling. If you work away from home during the day so that feeding and housebreaking are difficult, consider a three- to four-month-old puppy that is already trained and able to go longer without attention. If you are buying a show or breeding prospect, the more mature the dog, the surer the choice and, generally speaking, the higher the price. The proven, older brood bitch, the retired show dog that needs a new home, or the mature male that is ready to show may be just right for your situation. Don't shy away from such opportunities for fear the older dog will not adapt. It may take the older Beardie a little longer to accept you as his master, but he usually will adjust and make an ideal pet. Most breeders who place an older dog will do so on a trial basis.

Pet, Breeding, or Show?

Most breeders classify their Beardies in one of three basic categories—pet, breeding, or show prospects. One of the breeder's first questions is bound to be, "Do you want a show dog or a family dog?"

A Beardie sold as a pet is meant to be just that—a wonderful companion. He will look like a Beardie and will have the typical temperament and personality that may have prompted you to choose a Bearded Collie in the first place, but he will not have all the fine points of conformation necessary to qualify him for the show ring or breeding kennel. The pet Beardie is ideal for herding livestock and for competing in obedience work, tracking, or other practical work, and you won't need to be as concerned about his sustaining slight injuries or damaging his coat as you would if you used a show dog for this type of activity. (Yes, a show dog *can* do these things, too.)

The most important consideration in a pet is temperament. Even at weaning age, the young Beardie exhibits much of his adult personality. By watching a litter at play for a while, you can probably pick out the quietest, the boldest, the most aggressive, and the pup showing the strongest herding instinct. It is best not to select an extremely frightened or aggressive puppy

Breeding and show Beardies are very similar, if not identical, in quality. The young puppy is usually referred to as a "show prospect" because it is difficult to determine with total accuracy just how an eight-week or twelve-week puppy will mature. Exceptional Beardies that are six months of age or older may be classified as "show quality" and will be sold for higher prices than the young "prospects." At six months, the structure is evident, gait and coat are beginning to mature, and type is obvious. Because puppies may be shown at six months of age, the dog may even have begun to prove his mettle in the show ring. A show dog must be an excellent specimen of the breed, possessing all the qualities of temperament, personality, showmanship, and correct conformation that could make him a winner.

"Breeding quality" also denotes show quality or a Beardie that is only slightly less than perfect. The major difference is often the lack of poise or showmanship of the breeding-quality Beardie, especially in females. A dog purchased for breeding should have good temperament and good health and should exhibit no major faults. A show dog lamed by an injury or one that has lost an ear or a tooth or has been scarred in a fight may also be sold for breeding quality. (*See* Chapters 11 and 14 for more information on breeding and show-dog selection.)

WHERE DO YOU FIND YOUR DOG?

Finding the right Beardie may not be easy and it may take time, but he is well worth waiting for. If you can locate one or more breeders within driving distance, this is the place to start. You may also find Beardies exhibited at a local dog show (watch the ad column of your local newspaper for dates and places). You can probably locate breeders through your local kennel club referral service or by writing the American Kennel Club for the address of the parent club (the Bearded Collie Club of America). The BCCA can then send you a list of breeders. You may also find advertisements in national dog magazines (*see* "Other Sources").

A good way to develop an eye for a Beardie and to meet the breeders is to attend a dog show. Observe the judging carefully and ask a knowledgeable spectator to help you understand the reasons for the placements. After the breed has been judged, go quickly to the grooming area to discuss buying a puppy with a breeder/exhibitor whose Beardies attracted you. Most exhibitors are busy with preparations prior to ring-time but will be happy to talk with you immediately after the breed classes.

Before you actually make a purchase, try to visit the breeder at home. One clue to a good kennel is consistency of quality and type throughout the kennel, especially if evident through several generations. Another clue is the cleanliness and the kind of socialization and care provided. If overall type is varied or poor, temperaments are questionable, or kennel conditions unclean, look elsewhere.

What if you can't visit the breeder in person—can you still purchase a good Beardie? Yes, if you are careful. Rely on referrals from knowl-

*A playful older puppy owned by
Larry and Michelle Abramson.*

Hopefully, you will not find a Bearded Collie in a pet shop—a source that is definitely not recommended. Always buy from a breeder. Most breeders are reputable people who will help you select the right dog for your needs and become your friend and advisor while you are getting started in the breed. Some breed clubs maintain a rescue service—a placement service for older Beardies—that is worth looking into.

BEARDIE RESCUE

This is a very important function of the Bearded Collie Club of America, operating nationwide. Beardies that have been abandoned, abused, or left in shelters are taken in by volunteers and rehabilitated. Costs of veterinary care are paid from the Rescue Fund. Good homes are then found for these dogs. The director of this program is Paul Glatzer, (516) 724-0871. There are regional representatives throughout the country.

MAKING THE PURCHASE

Every AKC-registered dog should be sold with a signed litter or individual registration slip, a pedigree, and a sales contract that includes a guarantee. If the litter registration papers have not come back to the breeder from the AKC, the contract should contain a statement guaranteeing that they will be signed over to the purchaser as soon as they arrive. The seller may hold the registration certificate until certain contractual conditions such as neutering and payment completion are fulfilled.

The AKC has made available a limited registration that prevents any offspring of that animal from ever being registered. The sales contract should contain this provision. A dog with this registration cannot be shown in breed competition in a licensed or member dog show. He is eligible, however, to be entered in any other licensed or member event, such as obedience or herding.

edgeable handlers or judges or from breeders with an established reputation. Sometimes a professional handler will see and purchase a dog for you if you cannot travel in person. If you choose to write to breeders without a referral, take time to get to know them through letters or calls before you make a purchase

When you are buying a dog from another area of the United States, you often can have him shipped "on approval." Under these circumstances, you purchase the Beardie with an agreement that he may be returned for a full refund within a specified time period (usually a few days) if you find that the dog does not suit your requirements or feel that he was misrepresented. You pay all shipping expenses and assume responsibility for the dog while he is in your possession during the approval period.

SAMPLE SALES CONTRACT FOR PET PUPPIES

On (date) ———————————— XYZ KENNELS agrees to sell the following Beardie Collie

to: (name) ————————————————————————————————————

of: (address) ——————————————————————————————————

———————————————————— telephone: ————————————————

for the sum of $ ————————

Color: ————————————   Sire: ————————————————————

Sex: ——————————————   Dam: ———————————————————

Whelped: —————————————   Reg. #: ————————————————

REGISTRATION PAPERS:

1. Limited registration (non-breeding) papers will be given with the puppy (or will be transferred to the buyer immediately upon receipt from AKC if they are being processed) provided the animal has beenpaid for in full.

   OR

2. If the animal has not been fully paid for at the time it is transferred, limited registration papers will be held by the seller until payment has been made in full.

   OR

3. In the case of a pet bitch, the animal must be neutered before the registration papers are transferred. On receipt of a veterinarian's certificate that the bitch has been neutered, the limited registration papers will be transferred with no additional charge.

It is understood at the time of sale this dog is not considered to be of show or breeding quality, but it is representative of its breed and is structurally and temperamentally suited as a compaion or obedience or herding dog. Beginning training classes are highly recommended for any family dog to insure a happy relationship.

This dog is guaranteed for 48 hours against any health or temperament irregularities, and it is recommended the buyer have the puppy examined by a reputable veterinarian during this period. (Note: any puppy going to a new home may be a bit unsure of himself until he becomes familiar with his surroundings.) A full refund will be given for any pup found not satisfactory during the first 48 hours and returned in good condition. The buyer will be responsible for only shipping charges. No other guarantee is given or implied except in the case of an *hereditary* defect that develops (before the age of three years) to the extent that it renders the dog unsuitable as a pet. In this instance, a replacement will be given when one becomes available. Buyer will be responsible for only shipping charges.

Neutering of males is strongly recommended. Neutering of females is mandatory.

Special provisions: Signed: ————————————————————

                                       Signed: ————————————————————

                                       Address:————————————————————

                                       ———————————————————————————

                                       Telephone:——————————————————

Guarantees

Ask for and expect a written sales contract/guarantee. A pet generally will be guaranteed to be in good health for a specified period from date of purchase. He also may be guaranteed for good temperament and/or against any debilitating hereditary defects up to the age of two or three years. (This generally includes crippling dysplasia and blindness.)

A breeding-quality Beardie should carry a guarantee that the dog will be capable of reproducing, and either a show or breeding animal should be guaranteed against hereditary defects occurring before three years of age. Monorchidism, or cryptorchidism (failure of one or both testicles to descend into the scrotum), is a disqualification in any breed, and this should certainly be included in the guarantee on a show or breeding male.

Contracts for show Beardies may carry any number of terms. Some breeders guarantee that the dog will finish his championship. Others guarantee that the dog will be show quality by their definition at a certain specified age. The more protection you are given, the higher the price you can expect to pay.

Almost every registered Beardie should be sold with some type of contract to protect the buyer and seller. It is important that you understand and agree to these terms.

Payment Terms

There are many ways to buy a dog. The best and most usual is an outright cash purchase. A few large breeders will accept major credit cards or take time payments, in which case you will be asked to sign a contract and agree that the registration papers will be held by the seller until the last payment has been made.

"Breeder's terms" refer to the sale of a male with stud privileges (use of the dog for breeding retained by the seller) or the sale of a bitch with puppies or even litters to be given back to the seller. Sometimes exceptional show

Choosing the right puppy can be a difficult decision.

animals are sold this way to ensure that they and their offspring are properly bred and exhibited. Partial value of the puppies or litters is deducted from the sale price, and the bitch is usually co-owned until the payment in puppies has been fulfilled. If the terms are agreeable to both parties and the two individuals can work together reasonably, such arrangements can be advantageous to both. Terms must be spelled out in writing and clearly understood by both parties.

Permanent co-ownerships offer another method of obtaining a good Beardie. Co-ownerships may be offered by breeders who want to hold on to a Beardie for breeding but do not have the space or time to keep another dog. Some breeders will sell co-ownership only to a novice so that they can place the dog but essentially retain control and assure that the dog is shown, promoted, and bred properly. If the beginner is willing to cooperate with the experienced breeder, this may be an excellent way to obtain top-quality stock. Usually the person purchasing the co-ownership is expected to keep the dog. The two owners may split stud fees or litters, and the contract should specify in writing how this is done and who is to be responsible for maintenance, show, and advertising expenses.

Occasionally, it may be possible to lease a Beardie for a start in breeding without the permanency or expense of buying. Bitches are leased for a five- or six-month period, and the lease must be registered with the AKC. The lessee is generally responsible for the shipping charge, the stud fee, and all other expenses when leasing a bitch for a litter, or for the promotion costs and showing fees when leasing a stud dog. The lessee is held liable for the dog while the animal is in his care. About the only way to obtain a good Beardie on lease is to become acquainted with breeders and ask to be considered if they become interested in leasing a particular Beardie.

IMPORTING

Many of the Beardies in the United States at this time are either imported or are the offspring of imported dogs. The breed is relatively new to this country, and many breeders initially travelled to England in search of top-quality Beardies from the country of the breed's origin. Recently, some dogs have been imported from other countries as well as from England.

Importing, however, is expensive, risky, and not advisable for the novice breeder. A good puppy can be purchased in England for around $1,000, but the air fare, the duty, the crate, and the health certificate can greatly increase this amount. If you wish to import a dog, the best way is to make a trip to England and pick the dog after a tour of the major kennels. If you cannot do this, you may find an international judge who will select a good puppy for you.

Brave individuals may want to try writing to breeders in Great Britain and selecting their puppy by correspondence. Select a breeder who is well known or who has been recommended by another importer. A few English breeders want to send some of their best dogs out of the country, while others are concerned about not knowing what kind of home or promotion the dog will receive and are therefore reluctant to export their best.

The seller usually can arrange for transfer of papers and shipping. The airlines require that dogs be shipped in extremely large, heavy, usually wooden crates--hence the high freight rates. Upon entrance to the United States at either Los Angeles, Chicago, or New York City, the dog will be delayed for several hours for a health check. He then must clear customs at your nearest international airport.

Once the dog is here, he cannot be returned, so don't expect him to be shipped on approval. (Dogs going into England are kept in quarantine for six months.) Any guarantee for replacement will be strictly according to the charity of the breeder/seller. Because it is very difficult to purchase an adult, you will probably be importing a young puppy and therefore taking a greater risk in obtaining the quality you want.

The exporter must supply you with a three-generation export pedigree and British registration form for your dog. You must write to the American Kennel Club for an imported dog registration form. The AKC will instruct you how to apply for registration in this country.

5 The Comforts of Home

The first day at home with a new puppy is always enchanting. He will want to explore every corner, every door, every other animal, and, of course, every member of the family. His reactions may range from hilarious clowning to fright to a well-pulled-off bluff. You will hardly be able to take your eyes or hands off the lovely new creature. You will want to play with him, handle him, cuddle him, get acquainted, and, at the same time, reassure him.

But puppies, like babies, need time for sleep, and they do best if their mealtimes are quiet and undisturbed. You may want to keep your new Beardie closer to the family for the first few weeks while he's getting acquainted, but remember to allow him privacy and rest. His sleeping box, prepared before you bring him home, should be in a warm, draft-free corner away from the mainstream of family activities. A few rawhide chips or rawhide "bones," a Nylabone, a rubber ball, and a braid made of old nylon stockings will help entertain him and keep his teeth occupied on something other than dad's new slippers. A rug, old towel, or blanket provides comfortable bedding. If the box is large, you can prepare a bed at one end and spread papers for his toilet at the other end.

For the first few days in his new home, the best procedure is to let your Beardie become acquainted at his own pace. Don't push him to accept new sights, sounds, and experiences. He'll discover them in his own time and be much more confident than if he is rushed. As your puppy begins to feel at home, you can introduce him to all of the various aspects of his new life—car rides, hikes, other children, livestock, etc. Some Beardies will be hesitant and will need encouragement from you, while others will bounce right into anything and will need to be taught to heed your cautions.

Wybnellas River Pilot, "Baron," owned by Mr. and Mrs. F. Jaques.

The first month in a new home, especially for a two- to three-month-old puppy, is a very impressionable period in which the dog-owner bond is being formed. Take advantage of this period to form a relationship of mutual trust and respect with your Beardie.

EARLY TRAINING

Begin almost immediately to teach your Beardie what is expected of him. Even very young puppies are fully capable of learning, but their attention span is short. It is important to keep each lesson brief and to give lots of praise. A play period at the end is an excellent reward. If you are fortunate enough to have a Puppy Kindergarten class in your area, by all means enroll in it.

Discourage unruly behavior in the house by keeping your Beardie on a leash or confined to a small area at first. Discourage chewing on the wrong things, but because all puppies investigate their environment partly by chewing, provide him with rawhide or hard rubber toys. Praise him when he chews them. Never give him objects that he can easily tear into small pieces and swallow, except for rawhide.

Beardie puppies need to learn that you are the "boss." You will be off to a good start with your new relationship if you establish dominance, *without being harsh*. One way to establish dominance is to hold your puppy on his back while you talk sweetly to him. He probably will struggle, but keep him there until he lies still, then release him with lots of praise.

A very important lesson is the meaning of the word "NO," and some physical correction may be needed until this is learned. Tone of voice usually is sufficient correction. If not, you may discipline the puppy with a quick jerk on the collar, by picking him up by the scruff of the neck and shaking him, or by pushing his head to the ground and holding it there for a minute. Another good corrective measure is a swat with a rolled-up newspaper, but only if it is handy. *Corrections must be given within three seconds or not at all.* Always accompany the punishment with the command "No." Do *not* swat him with your hand.

Praise is the most important part of training. Always praise your Beardie lavishly when he performs as expected and as soon as he stops the behavior that you are correcting. If your Beardie is not responding well to your attempts at training, it may be that you are not giving him enough praise.

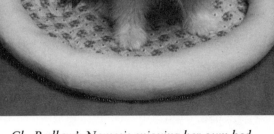

Ch. Bedlam's Nemesis enjoying her own bed. Courtesy Alice Bixler.

Come

You will probably also want to include the word "Come" in your puppy's early training. Call him to you often while he is with you in the house, rewarding him with praise and a goodie when he comes. If there are two people in the household, you can make a game by calling him back and forth between you. Don't be surprised, however, if your Beardie catches on so quickly that he runs back and forth without being called!

Housebreaking

Housebreaking can begin almost immediately, but don't expect your puppy to be perfectly dependable until he's at least three months old. In the beginning, it's up to you to anticipate when he has to relieve himself so that you can prevent accidents from happening.

The easiest method of housebreaking is to confine your puppy to a small area—a box, crate, or pen—at night. First thing in the morning, take him immediately to the area where you want him to relieve himself, and wait until

he does so. (It is best to avoid the intermediate step of paper breaking and take the puppy outside from the beginning.) Praise him immediately, then take him to the house for a romp. During the day when the puppy is inside, take him out to the same area whenever he is restless, when he wakes from a nap, shortly after a meal, or about every hour. The more vigilant you are in preventing accidents, the quicker he will learn. You will be surprised at how short a time it takes for him to become housebroken.

HOUSING

Beardies need space for exercise and play in order to keep their energy level manageable. If you must keep a Bearded Collie confined, allow time in your schedule for walks and romps in the open for at least an hour each day. If they are provided with this minimum requirement, Beardies adjust remarkably well to nearly any home

Although most Beardies are house dogs, some owners prepare a space in the yard or garage for their adult Beardies. A draft-proof doghouse or a raised, enclosed box in the corner of a garage or porch will do nicely for one or two dogs. Just remember that they still need their daily human companionship.

Crates

A Bearded Collie is much too active to be routinely confined to a crate. However, crate training can be a definite asset to any dog. There may come a time when your Beardie must be left at the veterinarian's office, stay with a friend, or be shipped to another location. The crate-trained dog will take this in stride.

Select a crate large enough for your Beardie to stand comfortably without ducking and to lie stretched out without being cramped. Wire crates are excellent for kenneling a dog in the house, but wooden or fiberglass crates are preferable for shipping. A shipping crate that is too large may cause the dog to be tossed about and possibly injured.

Crate training is easy. Simply put your Beardie in the crate for a short period at feeding time. Leave him there until he cleans up the food, then release him. This leads to pleasant associations and minimizes bad habits like scratching and whining. Gradually increase the confinement time to several hours or overnight. Give your Beardie a chew toy to alleviate boredom, but don't baby him. If he cries or claws at the crate, correct him immediately by scolding or by slapping the crate with a rolled-up newspaper. Your Beardie's ego is much tougher than he would like you to believe at times. In fact, a Beardie that continually gets his way will never really be well adjusted.

How much should you crate a Beardie? Opinions are varied. English breeders dislike crates and believe tnat much harm is done by using them. While this may be true in isolated incidents, there is a definite need for the use of crates in the United States. They are a necessity at unbenched dog shows; they provide safety while traveling in a car; and they furnish a clean, readily available in-house kennel where a Beardie can eat and sleep or be confined while you are entertaining, when you are out of the

house, or when you just don't want a dog underfoot. The maximum time for confining any dog to a crate is seven or eight hours. Obviously, the longer the period of confinement, the more conscientious you must be to provide exercise. If you have only one dog, do not assume that he will exercise himself, even in a large yard. Teach him to retrieve a ball or a Frisbee, or take him for long walks.

Kennels

If you intend to keep several Bearded Collies for breeding or show, you will undoubtedly want a kennel. There are as many kennel variations as there are breeders. Styles range from made-over poultry or livestock sheds to elaborately constructed custom buildings that architecturally harmonize with the home. Some are unheated, while others boast heating, air conditioning, and even septic systems.

Regardless of style or complexity, certain basics such as dryness, good ventilation, and sanitation must be met. You will also have to consider the zoning regulations imposed by your city, county, or state health department. Always check local regulations before you begin to build.

Either wood or cement-block building materials are acceptable. Wood is drier, but concrete is easier to disinfect and clean. With either material, place a layer of heavy plastic sheeting beneath the floor to keep out moisture.

The building should be well ventilated yet as draft free as possible. Louvered ventilator windows or fans near the roof at each end of the kennel will provide ventilation; in addition, you may want several screened windows above the dog boxes for air and light. Louvered mobile-home windows are excellent if you can obtain them. Another possibility, borrowed from poultry sheds, is to have windows at one end and a big exhaust fan at the other end.

The partitions between "stalls" should be sturdy, smooth, and about six feet high. A good size for stalls is four feet square, with a larger pen for a bitch and her puppies. Each stall

Fences should be six feet high if you plan to keep your Beardie confined. Ch. Meadows' New Kid on the Block doing what he does best. Courtesy Mary Billman.

should have an opening large enough to accommodate a grown Beardie. A swinging door or rubber flap will prevent drafts, and a guillotine-style door on the inside will keep the opening firmly closed when desirable. Commercial doors are available, or you can build your own by making a sliding wooden door and hanging a rubber automobile flap over the opening.

Runs should be at least 4 x 12 feet (4 x 24 feet would be better) with six-foot-high chain-link fencing. Concrete flooring, definitely the easiest to clean, is costly to install and will wear off the hair on your Beardie's feet and legs. Three-quarter-inch or the smaller "pea" gravel is preferred by many breeders

In either case, dig the area for the runs to a depth of at least sixteen inches. Lay a four- to six-inch layer of rock or very coarse gravel, and sprinkle it with Boraxo to help kill odors and worm larvae. Then lay the top surface with either fine gravel or concrete. The top half of the surface gravel will need replacing every couple of years for good sanitation.

Hard dirt runs or grass areas are difficult to keep clean, and because they encourage infestations of parasites, they are not recommended. You can get by with dirt or grass in a large exercise yard, but be aware that your grooming time will increase substantially if your Beardie is kept on these surfaces.

Sanitation

Cleanliness is essential in a kennel or any dog facility, and the more dogs you keep, the more important and time consuming this becomes.

Food and water dishes should be washed often. Hard-rubber or stainless-steel dishes resist damage and can be disinfected easily. Heavy ceramic bowls are also easy to clean and are nearly impossible to tip over, but be sure that they are made in the United States so that they do not contain lead. Soapy water with a little Clorox added is an old standby for any kennel owner. In addition to cleaning the dishes, use this solution to wash down the

Clean water, gravel, and chain-link fence provide safe kenneling for this Beardie puppy.
Ch. Willowmead Pollyanna.

building and runs several times a year. Commercial disinfectants are also available. Frequent spraying of runs with Clorox and water will help to control odors.

Pick up feces at least once daily. If flies, mosquitoes, or hookworms are a problem, remove the dogs and spray the premises with Malathion, following the instructions carefully. You must keep the dogs out of the area for twelve to twenty-four hours after spraying. Rock salt will aid in killing roundworm larvae. Sodium borate (commonly sold as Boraxo) applied at the rate of ten pounds per hundred square feet may be used to control hookworm larvae. Both substances can be harmful to the dog's feet and should be well raked into the gravel or applied to concrete and left on an empty run for a day and then washed off with water.

Disease control in the kennel is facilitated by placing a one-foot-deep concrete barrier at the base of the fencing between each run. If the runs are gravel, at least six inches of the barrier should be beneath the surface. A six- or eight-foot solid board fence around the periphery of the kennel is used by many commercial kennels to block airborne germs and noise. If you plan to raise, breed, or ship a number of dogs, a quarantine or isolation run removed from the rest of the kennel is essential. This run may be smaller than the others and should definitely have a concrete floor as well as an enclosed top for the safety of visiting Beardies.

KEEPING YOUR BEARDIE SAFE

In addition to the fact that you probably paid a lot of money for your Beardie, he is a living, breathing, cherished part of your family, and you want to do everything you can to protect him. Yet many purebred dogs die needlessly each year because their owners did not think about safety.

It seems like mere common sense to check your yard, kennel, or other facilities for holes or broken wires, cracks near a gate, insecure latches, and other precarious situations before you bring your dog home. Many new dog owners are not aware that a Beardie (or any dog) in a strange place can become a very adept escape artist. And because Beardies are quite capable jumpers, you will want to decide if your fences

Wybnellas River Pilot at home in Reading, England. Courtesy F. Jagnes.

are high enough. Any height less than six feet is questionable until your Beardie learns that this is his new home, after which he will probably stay inside fences over which he could easily leap.

While you are checking the premises, look also for chewable items such as accessible electrical cords, exposed fiberglass insulation, or other harmful or poisonous substances. Even adult dogs are likely to chew or swallow foreign objects; it is up to you to keep harmful items out of reach. In general, anything that might harm a child should also be kept away from your Beardie. Puppies are apt to tip things over, cut themselves on glass or tin, or step on sharp objects.

The Beardie's inborn herding tendencies can get him into a lot of trouble around livestock, so keep your dog away from stock unless he is supervised closely or is fully trained to work.

Although it seems unnecessary to warn you not to leave your Beardie locked in a closed car in summer, hundreds of dogs die annually of heat stroke from this very cause. When outside temperatures approach 80 degrees, the inside of your automobile will register more than 100 degrees.

Poisonous Substances

Many common items are poisonous to dogs if ingested. Among these are chlorine bleach, antifreeze, cleaning fluid, gasoline, fungicides, insecticides, herbicides, rat poisons, tar, suntan lotion, wax, paint and paint removers, hair-setting lotions, hair-coloring lotions, matches, mothballs, shoe polish, children's crayons, some household detergents, disinfectants, aspirin, and other drugs.

It is best to keep all house plants away from your Beardie. Many of them are poisonous to dogs, including dieffenbachia, philodendron, poinsettia, and mistletoe. Gardeners should also be concerned that many bulbs, vines such as wisteria, bittersweet, and sweet peas, and bushes such as euonymus, rhododendron, laurel, and yew can be harmful to your dog. Castor beans, especially the seed, are extremely poisonous.

Tattooing

Dognapping has become so common that any dog in any community is a potential victim. Tattooing is inexpensive and painless and takes only a few minutes. It can be done by a veterinarian or at one of the many tattoo clinics held in conjunction with dog shows and matches. Microchips are also becoming a popular method of identification. The chip is implanted under the dog's skin by a veterinarian.

Your social-security number (or another number such as your dog's AKC registration number) is tattooed permanently on the inside of your Beardie's right thigh. Always keep this area clipped so that the tattoo is readily visible. (Tattooing on the lip or ear is not recommended.) Tattooing or microchips are the only acceptable, positive legal identification recognized by law-enforcement authorities.

This number, along with your name, address, and telephone number, may be registered with the National Dog Registry (NDR), a nationwide organization that aids in the identification of lost, stolen, or stray dogs. Any dogs that you own are tattooed with the same number, and a notice is sent to the NDR. The listing lasts for a lifetime. (If you use the AKC number, each dog must have a separate number and a separate NDR listing and fee.) If your dog is lost, there is a very good chance that he will be returned to you because state and local police, humane societies, and more than 1,500 research labs, medical schools, and other organizations that work with dogs have been asked to verify through the NDR any dog that is delivered to them bearing a tattoo

The NDR also provides a name tag that your dog should wear any time he travels. The tag warns, "Tattooed dog registered with NDR." Similar warning signs are available for your car, crates, and kennel. For information and registration forms contact the National Dog Registry.

The AKC now requires positive identification of each dog if you own more than one of the same breed and sex. This can be done by adding a separate code to your social-security number,

such as your initial plus a number. The first dog would show P-1, the next P-2, etc. Your number plus the code should be written on each dog's AKC registration certificate in your file.

FINDING A LOST BEARDIE

If your Beardie wanders or becomes lost, there are a number of steps you can take to help locate him. Number one—don't panic! A high percentage of lost dogs are eventually returned to their owners.

If your dog becomes frightened and simply runs away, try to 'keep him in sight *without* making him feel that he is being pursued. As soon as he calms down, he probably will respond to your call. If he doesn't, try running away from him and he often will follow. Or try sitting down on the ground with your back to him and calling him. If several people are available to help, you can often corner your fleeing dog against a fence or building.

If your Beardie disappears and you can't sight him, act quickly. First call the local humane society, the dog-control officer, and your local radio station, giving a complete description of your dog and the place where you last saw him. Leave your name and phone number, along with the name and number of a friend who can be reached in case you are out. If the dog is newly purchased, contact the old owner in case your Beardie tries to return to his former home. Run an ad in the paper, offering a reward for information leading to your dog's return.

In case your dog is injured, call any veterinarians in your general region, then begin a house-to-house inquiry covering the entire area where your dog was last seen. Ask these residents to call you if your dog is sighted, and to please not chase him themselves. This keeps your dog from becoming more frightened, and he probably will seek water and shelter instead of continuing his flight.

Another possibility is to have fliers printed with your dog's description and a picture if available. These can be posted around the area and handed out to school children or other groups. You also might contact mailmen or meter readers who work in the area. Go to the local humane society or pound daily, rather than just calling, and show a picture of your Beardie. Be patient; many dogs are found after one, two, or even more weeks away from home.

THE JET-SET BEARDIE

About as many dogs as people travel these days. If your Beardie is accustomed to going along on family outings, to visiting relatives, and to taking jaunts down to the ice-cream parlor from the time he is a puppy, he will eagerly anticipate an automobile ride. On the other hand, if the only place you ever take him is to the vet's for a vaccination or to a few shows now and then,

he'll probably be nervous and may even get carsick. It is far better to start him out slowly at a young age with a few rides to the store or around the block. If he still has a tendency to get carsick, a Drammamine™ tablet given about thirty minutes before departure may help.

If you are going on a long trip with your Beardie, or if he will be flying, make sure that he is wearing a collar with an ID tag, rabies tag, and tattoo notice. Don't feed him for twelve hours before traveling, and withhold water two hours before departure. (If he is flying, follow the airline rules about food and water.) Feed and water him only lightly during the trip. It is always a good idea to take plenty of his regular food and drinking water, because unfamiliar food and/or water easily cause digestive upsets. It helps to have a bag containing plenty of newspapers, paper towels, a

"Are we there yet?" Life in a motor home. Courtesy M. Billman.

washcloth, Drammamine, Kaopectate, and a laxative or suppository. This will prepare you for almost anything.

If you will be crossing state lines, take a health certificate and rabies vaccination tag or papers. You may never have to show them, but it may save you time and trouble. If you are going into Canadaor Mexico, they are required.

Shipping by Air

Thousands of dogs fly throughout the United States each year with relative ease and safety. New regulations make air-freight shipments even safer than before. Anyone involved in breeding or showing Beardies extensively will one day ship a dog by air.

Proper preparation helps to ensure your Beardie a safe trip. The basics are simple:

1. Make reservations with the appropriate air-freight office several days in advance. *Choose a nonstop, direct flight* if possible. If a transfer is necessary, allow plenty of time for it. Ask the freight agent about regulations regarding type of crate and air temperatures at point of takeoff and destination. If it is too hot or too cold, your dog may have to wait until a more moderate day.
2. Prepare the crate. *Be sure that the size is comfortable but not too large.* Spread a layer of newspapers on the floor, topped by a second layer of shredded paper. Apply a label that notes "Live Dog. Do Not Place Near Dry Ice. Do Not Open Crate Except in Emergency." Prepare a shipping label prominently displaying the name, address, phone number, city, and airport to which the dog is being shipped, as well as your name, address, and phone number.
3. *Obtain a health certificate.* Interstate-commerce regulations require that all dogs crossing state lines be checked by a veterinarian within ten days or so (depending on the state) and certified to be in good health. A current rabies vaccination is required. To avoid overstressing your Beardie, take him in for the examination a day or two before shipment.

The freight office will request that you have your dog at the airport about two hours before takeoff to allow adequate time for safe and correct loading. Always place a collar (not a choke collar) with ID tag on your Beardie before shipment, and put only one dog in each crate. Exercise your dog just before leaving him at the airport.

At the airport, check the air bill carefully to make sure that all information and phone numbers are correct. You might watch the agent place the air bill on the crate to make certain that the correct air bill goes with the dog. Unless you declare a value and insure your dog, the airline will pay only a minimum figure in case of loss, so be sure to buy insurance.

Your dog will be placed in the crate and weighed. If you wish, double-check the latch, then leave the rest to the airline. You should remain available, either at the airport or near your phone at home, until takeoff in case some emergency would prevent shipment. As a final precaution, always request that the receiving person phone to let you know that your dog has arrived safely at his destination.

Flying With Your Beardie

Most of the same requirements will apply. You must make a reservation for your dog, have a health certificate and rabies vaccination, and a proper-size crate. You will take your dog to the passenger check-in rather than to the freight office. You will need to pay an excess baggage charge. If you are flying with a very small puppy, it may be possible to take him into the cabin with you, but ask the airline about this.

If possible, watch to see that your dog is loaded into the plane before you take your seat. If you can't do that, ask the flight attendant to check with the pilot to see if your dog is on the plane. This is your right, so be firm about it.

6 The Beardie Beautiful

It is important for breeders to impress upon prospective Beardie owners that coat care is a major factor to consider. As an owner you must be willing to spend the time and effort for proper grooming or be prepared to take your dog to a professional groomer regularly. A third option is to keep your dog in a kennel or utility clip. Thorough grooming is important, not only for appearance, but for the health and comfort of your Beardie.

The Bearded Collie is a "natural" breed, which means that no obvious trimming or sculpturing of the coat is allowed. Just what is consistent with good grooming can be quite a borderline decision. Obvious sculpturing, such as is done on the neck, tail, and belly line of setters, on the feet of Cocker Spaniels, and on the knitting-needle parts of Shih Tzus, certainly goes way beyond grooming and is to be abhored, because it completely destroys the natural look. On the other hand, hair sometimes grows in such a way that it makes a dog look bad when he really isn't, and it could be argued that a bit of judicious trimming would be merely good grooming. A clean, healthy, well-brushed dog can grace the show ring or present his best appearance as a pet.

TOOLS AND EQUIPMENT

Requirements for grooming tools are minimal. The most important item is a good-quality bristle brush. Do not economize on this tool. If possible, get a Mason-Pearson bristle or bristle-and-nylon brush. These come in a variety of sizes and, though high in price, are a good investment because they last for years, will keep

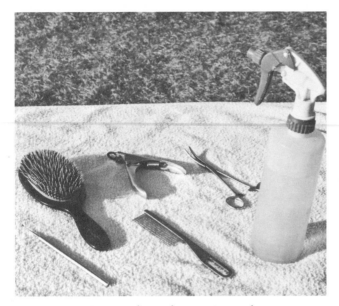

Commonly used grooming tools.

maintain and produces the typical *shaggy* outline. The formula for cultivating a beautiful coat is simply to keep it clean, healthy, and brushed. Assuming the coat has adequate genetic potential, it will develop length and shine in direct proportion to how much effort you exert. An adult pet needs to be brushed thoroughly only once a week. Depending on the dog, his environment, and the efficiency of your technique, this will take from fifteen minutes to an hour

Puppies tend to develop coat in one of two distinct manners. The first type of coat is rather sparse, wiry, and not overly attractive in the puppy stages. This type, however, is usually worth waiting out, because the adult coat will come in very harsh, easy to groom, and with a tendency to fall perfectly into place and stay there. Many of the more glamorous puppies

the coat in beautiful condition, and will cut your grooming time. If you can't justify the cost, get the best brush that you can afford. In addition, get a pin brush with stainless-steel bristles, a slicker brush, a wide-toothed comb, and a medium-toothed comb. The slicker brush is good for removing loose undercoat during a shed, the pin brush works well for routine brushing of pets, and the bristle brush is for finishing. Only use the bristle brush for grooming a show dog.

Add to your list three general-care items—a nail clipper, a tooth scaler, and a long forceps for plucking hair from the ear canal. For bathing your Beardie, get a good brand of dog shampoo, a bottle of liquid bluing, perhaps some coat conditioner if you live in a dry climate, a bottle of shampoo formulated for use on white hair, and a few old towels. If you become an expert, you may want to add a few extras of your own, but remember that a natural look is an essential element of Beardie type. There are plenty of breeds available for the frustrated hairdresser; the Beardie is *not* one of them.

EVALUATING THE COAT

The correct coat for the Bearded Collie is moderate in length, harsh in texture, and easy to

An ungroomed Beardie — the original "shaggy dog." Courtesy Sterling.

actually have soft, wooly coats verging on Old English Sheepdog type. This is alright in a *puppy*, but the coat should change in character until there is less undercoat and a long, harsh, straight outer coat by the time the dog is three years old.

Surprisingly, the profuse puppy coats are more difficult to keep up than the adult coats, because they tangle more easily and require more frequent brushing. Likewise, an incorrect adult coat, tending toward that of either the Old English Sheepdog or the Afghan Hound, will be much more difficult to groom and will need constant attention to look neat. The Old English coat may be curly and carry too much undercoat for a Beardie. The Afghan-type coat is usually dead straight but silky and limp to the touch. Either coat, though sometimes glamorous, is absolutely incorrect for a Beardie.

The Beardie coat has one unusual feature. Like human hair, it will continue to grow unless it is cut or broken off.

TABLE MANNERS

You may groom on a standard grooming table, on a portable top placed on a crate, on a card table with nonslip footing added, or even on the floor (this is suitable only for routine brushing of a well-trained animal). Table training definitely takes the work out of grooming and has other applications as well. It can provide a simple, impressive means of showing off your dog. On the table, he looks animated and unrestrained, yet he is confined to keep him from becoming pushy or overbearing to people.

Start putting your puppy on the grooming table when he is young, and get him accustomed to lying down while being brushed. All puppies and new adult Beardies try to jump off, but attempt to prevent this until your dog reliably understands what is expected. If he does escape, grab him, add a sharp verbal "No," and lift him backward onto the table. Then give him a Stay or Wait command and plenty of praise. Your dog must be praised for obeying even if you are forcing him to obey; otherwise, he has no incentive to do as you ask. If you know that your dog is thinking about jumping off, correct him before he actually leaps. Be sure to praise him. He should *never* jump off of a grooming table (or out of a car) until given the command to do so. Most dogs love their table and never resent this training once they understand what is wanted.

If you want the convenience of having your dog jump onto the table, this is how to teach

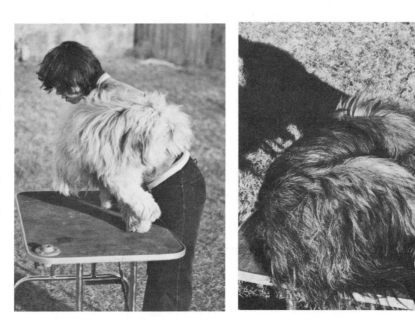

Right: Lift the dog and gently lay him on his side.

Far Right: Hold the feet until the dog stops struggling and will lie quietly on his side.

him. Do this exercise only with an adult dog that is already trained to lie on the table. Always lift puppies and pregnant bitches both on and off the table.

With your dog on lead, use the command "Up" and pat the table. He may put his front feet up the first time. If he does this, praise him lavishly and lift his hindquarters onto the table. If your dog isn't inclined to listen, talk in a happy, excited voice, repeating "Up" as you drag him onto the table by the collar. After you have pulled him up once, try again, leaving the lead slack and giving him a chance to do it himself. He'll probably be hesitant, so praise is most important. If he turns away, jerk him back. After a few times, he'll jump eagerly onto the table

The command "Up" is useful to get Beardies onto other objects besides tables, such as the platform used at shows for photographing group wins. It never hurts to think positively. You never know when you'll need it.

"Down Boy, Down"

Grooming is decidedly easier if your Beardie will lie on his side and allow you to brush him. In fact, it is the *only* way to thoroughly groom the underside of a Beardie single-handedly. With the dog on his side, you can probably groom him completely in the time it takes to whisk over the top while he is standing.

To teach him, stand him on the table and face his side. Encircle him with your arms approximately at hock level and clasp your hands together. In one motion, lean your body into his and pull his feet toward you. Try to lay him gently onto his side rather than throwing him like a rodeo calf. He will probably struggle and may become panicky for a few moments. Talk to him soothingly and keep him pinned with your body until he relaxes. Once he feels limp, rest a hand on his neck to steady him, then straighten up. Brush him lightly for a few minutes, then allow him to stand. Again, use a specific command to allow your dog to stand up. Repeat it a few times, and he will soon learn to get up and lie down on command, or at least remain passive as you place him in position.

If your dog tries to get up, hold his head flat on the table and repeat the Stay command. He will not be able to get up unless he maneuvers his legs on the bottom side underneath himself, and he is unlikely to manage this unless he raises his head. Grasp his foreleg on the underside in one hand and his corresponding hind leg in your other hand. Pull until his legs are straight toward you and your dog is again flat on his side. You can then begin brushing. You may either stand (this is preferable at first because you may have to steady your dog) or pull up a chair and sit down while grooming. To help keep your dog relaxed, keep up a steady stream of chatter, relieving his boredom and making it a game.

THE GROOMING PROCESS

The single technique that must be learned for grooming Beardies is called line-brushing. This is a method of separating the coat into sections and brushing against the lay of the hair until the entire dog has been brushed. The hair must be brushed clear to the roots to separate the undercoat and remove dead hair. A dog that is line-brushed completely once a week should sport a healthy, well-groomed coat. (A damaged coat may need more frequent attention, preferably daily brushing with the addition of some coat oil in the spray during the conditioning period.)

With your dog lying on his side, spray the entire coat lightly with water. You will also spray every four or five inches along the line of brushing as you progress along the body. Start on your dog's muzzle and brush a few hairs at a time forward over his nose. Advance toward his neck, brushing a few more hairs with each stroke. It helps to hold the unbrushed hair with your free hand and slide this hand ahead of the brush as you progress.

If you come upon a mat or piece of tangled hair, separate it with your fingers and brush it apart. If necessary, insert the end tooth of your

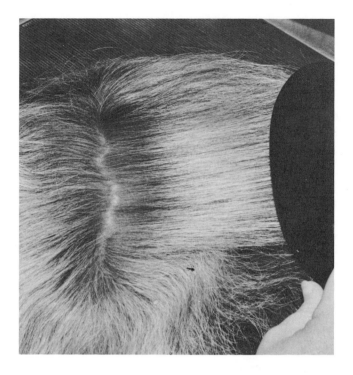

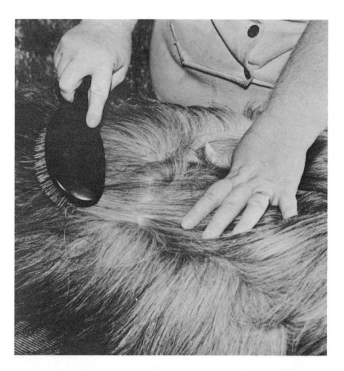

Top left: Separate the coat into sections.

Top right: Linebrushing.

Middle left: Pluck hair growing over the inside corner of the eye.

Middle right: Whisk the coat back into place.

Bottom: Comb the whiskers down and the beard forward.

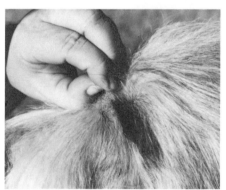

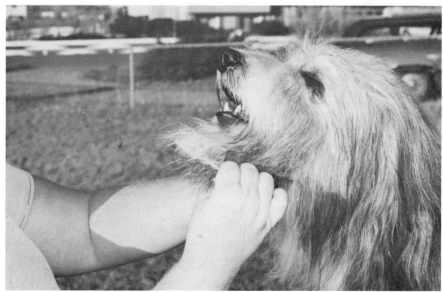

comb and split the tangle, then loosen it with your fingers and comb it out. If you take your time, even the worst mats will come out without your cutting or tearing a hole in the coat. Weekly brushing will prevent formation of any but the most insignificant tangles, and if your Beardie has correct coat texture, he will rarely mat.

Half of the grooming should take place between the nose and the withers. Areas of very dense hair growth under the ears and on the sides of the neck are often overlooked. Lift the ear up so that the underside is exposed. Line-brush under the line of attachment of the ear from muzzle to neck. Don't worry if you can't reach the whole beard. You are to groom only half of the dog from this side, and you will need to touch up areas later.

Separate and brush the hair on the inside of the ear, and check to see if any hair is growing inside the ear canal. If you find hair, pluck it out carefully following the technique described at the end of this chapter. Next, place the ear back in its normal position and brush the outside fringes. Start at the middle of the skull (remember, you're grooming half of the dog) and line-brush to blend with the completed area. Progress back along the neck. If you have a dog with profuse undercoat, you may want to rebrush this area at right angles to the original brush lines. You will see the difference in the finished look and in the lack of mats behind the ears. Before going any farther, brush the hair away from your dog's eyes and nose. He will lie much more patiently if he can watch what's happening. If you have trouble getting through the coat on a puppy, remember that he will become easier to groom as the coat matures.

Next, separate the coat vertically from the middle of the back downward along the edge of the brushed area. Spray one squirt of water along this line and continue brushing. Always move toward the rear of the dog. The coat is still being brushed toward the head, with the brush moving up and down the part and including slightly more hair in each stroke. The body area will be easy to maintain once it has been initially groomed. Repeat the pattern from top to bottom along the dog's side until you reach the loin area.

Now go back and do the front leg. Lift the leg and brush the chest hair and the area around the elbow. Spiral down and around the leg, spraying and line-brushing as you go. Brush the hair on the leg straight up toward the body. Separate this hair thoroughly, paying special attention to the elbow and toes. Brush clear to the tips of the toes, using the comb to separate the undercoat whenever necessary. Examine the toenails to determine if they need clipping. (*See* the end of this chapter for instructions.) Next, continue your line-brushing across the hip and down the hind leg. Be sure to separate all of the hair in the skirts (the long hair behind the thigh). When this is completed, turn your dog over and repeat the procedure for the other side. It is easier if you have your dog's legs toward you as you groom.

When this is finished, have your dog stand and line-brush down the center of his back. The mature coat should fall into a natural part. You may wish to brush the hair down each side to encourage this but do *not* part the back with a comb or other tool. Let your dog shake, then lightly whisk all hair back down into its natural lay.

Next, go to the front of your dog and start line-brushing, working downward on his chest from his throat. Brush the hair upward, but progress down the chest with the brush. When you are finished, whisk this hair back down also. Then work from the throat to the chin and separate every hair in the beard. You will probably have to comb the beard and face as a finishing touch. The sides of the muzzle are combed down, the top of the skull is combed straight back from the eyes, and the beard is combed forward. The only part left is the tail, which is simply line-brushed around and around from base to tip, with the feather brushed back into its natural plume. You may need someone to hold the dog if he objects to having his tail brushed. When you're finished, he will probably shake. The hair can then be whisked back into position.

Bathing

A Beardie should be bathed only when necessary and at least five days prior to a show so that the texture can return to the coat. The white parts will have to be rebathed the day before the show.

The most important step in bathing your Beardie is to give him a *thorough* line-brushing from head to toe, regardless of how dirty he is. If you bathe your dog unbrushed, the undercoat will pack tightly against his body and create a solid mat. Brushing him out afterwards will then be more difficult and will tear out considerably more undercoat. The anal glands can be emptied immediately before a bath so that any residue can be washed off. (Refer to the end of the chapter for details.)

Set out your towels, shampoos, bluing, and a container for mixing. A hand-held spray attachment is extremely helpful and can be purchased to fit almost any shower head. Stand your dog in the tub and wet him thoroughly. Start at the neck and work backward, leaving the head for last.

Work some shampoo into the hair around the neck, then lather along the back, down the legs, and finally around the skirts and tail. Let the soap set for two or three minutes, then rinse. Work through the coat with your fingers as you rinse to be sure that the soap is washing out completely. Wet the hair on the skull, ears, and muzzle, being careful to avoid the eyes and ear canal. Rub a small amount of shampoo between your palms and wipe it over the skull and ears. The beard and muzzle should then be thoroughly washed with a shampoo formulated for white hair. After the head is carefully rinsed, lather the feet, the tip of the tail, and the chest with the whitener shampoo. Rinse and repeat if necessary until these areas are clean.

If the coat is dry, a creme rinse or a diluted oil-base conditioner may be helpful. Do not apply creme rinse just before a show, because it softens the coat. As a final touch, rinse the white parts with a bluing solution. Use just enough bluing to color the water sky blue—roughly eight to ten drops to two quarts of water. The hair will dry a sparkling white.

Squeeze excess water from the coat and rub your dog's head with a dry towel. Blot water from the body coat and rub the legs briskly. Allow your dog to shake. When he is partially dry, line brush his coat throughly, and repeat when he is completely dry. The line-brushing will go very rapidly if you brushed your dog properly before bathing.

You can encourage the hair to part and fall to each side in a natural manner. While your Beardie is still wet after his bath, part the hair down the middle of his back, using a comb. When he is dry, brush the hair toward the tail, and then let him shake. The hair should fall to the sides without an exact part.

Chalking

Some exhibitors just brush and show their dogs. Others work a "chalk" powder into the slightly damp legs and whiskers for whitening and texture. Grooming chalk, cornstarch, calcium carbonate, or a mixture of these elements are used most frequently. After it dries, all chalk must be brushed out. No artificial substance should remain in the coat when the dog enters the show ring, and, in fact, is grounds for disqualification.

Grooming the Show Dog

Grooming the show Beardie takes more time and care. You must spray and brush your dog daily using only a bristle brush, because any other will tear the coat. The Beardie Standard states that the dog should be shown as naturally as is consistent with good grooming, but the coat must not be trimmed in any way. Unfortunately, trimming for the ring has become more and more common. The difference between "good grooming" and "trimming" is a fine line indeed, and to an extent, it is a personal decision. Good grooming, however, should leave a Beardie looking natural and *never* looking sculptured. If a handler is showing the dog, it is the responsibility of the owner to insist that the dog look natural

The hair on the feet can be so long that the dog is tripping over it. Often, the hair grows longer to one side so that the feet look crooked when they really are not. In these cases, the feet certainly are in need of proper grooming. To avoid a "trimmed" look, try the following. Stand your dog on the grooming table. Comb the hair outward around the leg and foot. Using forty-six-tooth thinning shears, hold them pointing downward, parallel to the leg. Cut in this position around the foot, trimming the hair back to about the same distance as the leg hair grows. Do not cut around the foot with the scissors parallel to the table.

Your Beardie may have an excess of undercoat in one or more places that can make him look unbalanced. A fine stripping knife can thin out some of the undercoat. Work from underneath so that the outer coat will not be affected. Use the stripping knife as if it were a comb, combing down against your thumb with a slight twist of your wrist. Take out just a little bit at a time and keep combing to judge your progress.

Brush out your dog completely, ready for the ring, before preparing the head. It's easier to do with your dog lying on the table.

Start with the hair on the backskull brushed back (Photo 1). Use a comb to create a triangle from one outside corner of the eye to the other (Photo 2). Comb the hair forward, hairspray the roots of the section, then backcomb close to the roots (Photo 3). If you have an exceptionally good head, this is all that you will need to do — just enough to keep the hair out of the eyes. If the head could use a little help, make several more sections parallel to the first, repeating the process. It may even be necessary to do a little backcombing on the sides just below and behind the eyes, depending on the individual head that you are grooming. Carefully smooth the hair back from the eyes with your hands (Photo 4) and *lightly* go over it with a brush. Put a little hairspray on your index finger and run this up the stop, then lightly go over it all with the hairspray. It should *not* feel stiff. Hold the head until the spray dries and *voilá*, a beautifully groomed head that stays that way (Photo 5). Do not go overboard and make the head look overdone (Photo 6). Afterward, carefully remove the backcombing, spray with water to dilute the hairspray, and condition.

If You Are Not Showing Your Beardie

Trimming to make your dog easier to care for is perfectly alright. He will track in less mud or debris if his feet are trimmed closely. To keep hair out of his eyes, you can use a barrette or you can trim the hair over his eyes into slightly overhanging eyebrows. He can even be clipped all over, although he will lose some of "Beardie look." It is best if the hair is left about an inch long rather than being clipped to the skin. His face can be clipped into a terrrier style with whiskers and eyebrows, and the hair on his tail either left long or trimmed about two-thirds of its length with the end plume left. If you have a groomer doing the clipping, be sure to talk it over first and explain exactly what you want so that there are no unpleasant surprises

ROUTINE CARE

The following procedures should be performed at regular intervals. It is best to set up a schedule so that they are not neglected. A well-cared-for dog will live a longer, happier life and will have fewer problems over the years.

Ear Care

Any hair growing from the ear canal should be removed. If left, it can form an air blockage and contribute to ear infections. If you do not have a long forceps, pluck as much hair as you can reach with your fingers. This will help but will not remove hair that extends into the canal. This hair is not anchored, and plucking is not painful to your dog. If you have forceps, *carefully* reach as far as possible into the canal and clamp onto the hair. Do not reopen the forceps, but twist around and around until all of the hair

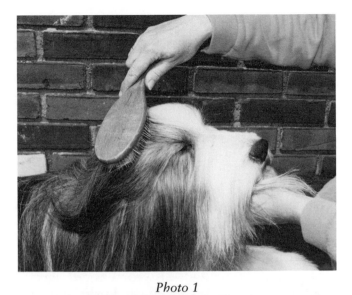

Photo 1

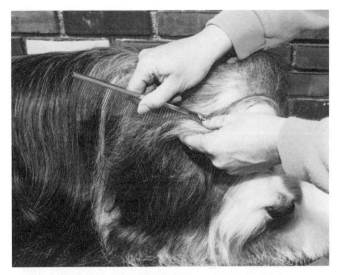

Photo 2

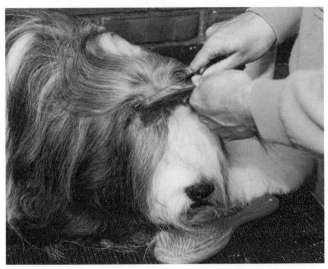

Photo 3

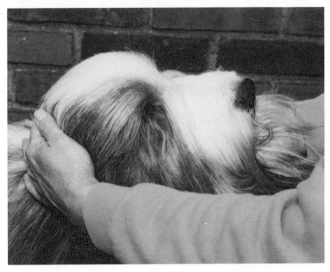

Photo 4

Photo 5

Photo 6

Pluck hair from the ear canal.

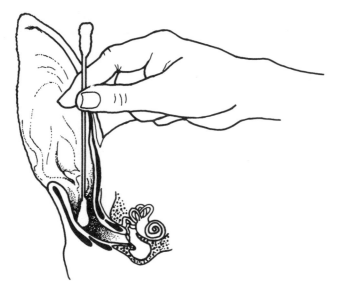

Figure 6-1
Carefully clean the visible portion of the ear canal with a cotton swab.

pulls loose. Repeat if necessary. If you are still uncertain about this procedure, have a vet or a good groomer show you how easy it actually is.

Occasionally, you will want to clean your Beardie's ears. Use rubbing alcohol on a cotton swab. Do not worry about alcohol getting into the canal—it will assist in wax removal and will evaporate harmlessly. Clean only the visible surfaces with your swab; never probe into the canal. If your dog scratches his ears continuously, shakes or tilts his head a great deal, or cries out when his ears are touched, he may have ear mites, an infection, or a foreign object imbedded in the ear. Have a vet check your dog if you suspect any of these problems.

Toenails

Toenails should be clipped at least every two weeks unless your dog is very active and wears down his nails on a hard surface. Long toenails cause the foot to spread or splay, making footing difficult. Long nails also force the weight of the body onto the heel of the pad instead of distributing it evenly, resulting in tender, broken-down feet and pasterns.

If your dog's dewclaws (fifth toe located on the inside of each front leg, almost at the pastern) have not been removed, be sure to clip them. They do not wear down like the nails on the feet do and can grow in a complete circle and back into the leg in time. Dewclaws are particularly dangerous on Beardies because the breed is active and prone to tearing the claws

Figure 6-2
Trim the nails almost to the quick.

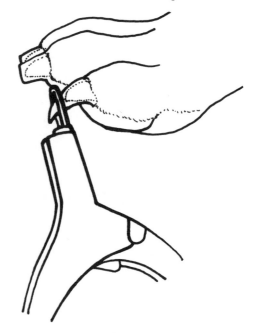

off in the underbrush. Also, the coat on the legs hides the dewclaws from view so that they are easily forgotten and allowed to grow too long

Hold the foot as illustrated and cut the nail almost to, but not into, the blood line (the pink center of the nail). If you cannot see the quick, remove only the hooked portion of the nail and you will not cut too deeply. After the nail is trimmed, the blood line will recede somewhat as your dog brings his foot in contact with the ground; conversely, in a nail that has not been trimmed for some time, the quick will grow longer so that it reaches close to the tip of the nail. Because such a nail cannot be cut back as far as it should be with the first trimming, you will have to cut only a tiny bit, then repeat the process every few days until the nail has been trimmed back to the proper length. If you cut too deeply, the nail will bleed but the injury is not serious. A little styptic powder or Kwik Stop will control the bleeding. Your Beardie may remember and be a little touchy about his feet at the next grooming session, however. The properly trimmed nail should just clear the floor when the dog is standing on a hard surface

There are several kinds of nail clippers, and all of them work well. Most breeders prefer the type illustrated here. When your nail clippers become so dull that the nail is pinched or crushed instead of cut, it is time to buy a new pair. Always hold the clipper with the handle *below* the nail, tilting slightly backward. Cutting with the clipper to one side or on top tends to crush the nail rather than make a clean cut.

Foot Care

Because of the requirement for leaving hair between the toes, be sure to check thoroughly for grass seed and stickers, which can become imbedded in the foot. The hair actually protects against the majority of foreign bodies, but those that persevere are harder to detect and may be more easily overlooked than on a trimmed foot. If neglected, they can cause a serious infection.

"Cheat-grass" seed or foxtails are the worst offenders. In areas where these weeds predominate, it may be necessary to comb your Beardie's feet daily or, if he is not being shown, some trimming between the pads may be warranted.

Sore pads are fairly common in any active breed. They can be caused by excessive dryness or cracking, by a bruise, or from too much running on hard or uneven surfaces. Salt used to thaw ice in winter or kill worms in gravel runs may also cause sore feet. There are several commercial preparations such as Tuf-Foot or Pad-Kote that you may apply, or just try a little petroleum jelly or hand lotion to heal the cracks. Splinters or other foreign objects in the pad can usually be removed with a tweezer. Swab the area with rubbing alcohol, remove the splinter, then apply first-aid cream.

Teeth

Like humans, dogs need the tartar removed from their teeth in order to avoid gum disease. Puppies generally clean their teeth by chewing, but most adult dogs need assistance, especially as they grow older. Dogs that have had their teeth scaled regularly are less likely to lose their teeth with age. Rawhide chews, Nylabones, dry kibble, and other products made especially for this purpose are helpful, but if you check your Beardie's teeth at each of your weekly checkups, you will probably find some buildup of discoloring tartar

Your vet can remove this tartar for a significant fee that usually includes anesthesia, but if you are economy-minded, buy a tooth scaler and train your puppy to allow you to do the job yourself. If done regularly, cleaning takes only a few minutes. A good-quality, sharp scaler, obtainable from your dentist, your vet, or a dog-supply catalog, is essential

Begin with the upper incisors. Hold the lip away from the teeth with one hand and, with the other hand, use the scaler to scrape from just under the edge of the gum downward. Use short, firm strokes, cleaning only a small area of

Tartar must be scaled from teeth regularly.

Occasionally, these glands become clogged, accumulating a foul-smelling mass. Irritation of the glands results.

Clogging may be caused by injury to the region, by bacterial infection, or by migration of segments of tapeworm into the ducts of the glands. Obesity and lack of muscular tone may be contributing factors in old dogs. Chronically soft feces will also cause retention of the fluid. Closely confined dogs appear to have more difficulty than active dogs.

The most common early sign of anal irritation is when the dog licks or bites at the perineum. As the condition progresses, the dog may drag his anus across the floor or rub it against any rough surface. This action almost always indicates that the anal glands need to be emptied rather than that the dog has worms (as the old wives' tale would have us believe). If the glands

the tooth with each stroke. Be careful not to jab the tongue or lower jaw as you pull downward, but use enough pressure to chip the tartar loose.

After you have cleaned all of the upper teeth on both inside and outside surfaces, including the molars in the back of the mouth, repeat with the bottom teeth, scraping from the gum upward. Rinse the scaler in an oral antiseptic several times during the process. Complete the job by polishing the teeth with powdered pumice or toothpaste on a soft cloth. Several brands of toothpaste flavored to appeal to dogs are available from pet suppliers.

If your Beardie has bad breath even though his teeth are clean, try swabbing his teeth and gums with baking soda or Happy Breath. Strong, persistent breath odor may indicate that your dog has abscesses or that he has poor digestion or other health problems. Call this to the attention of your veterinarian at your Beardie's next checkup.

Anal Glands

These two small glands located below and on either side of the anus secrete a lubricant that enables the dog to expel his feces more easily.

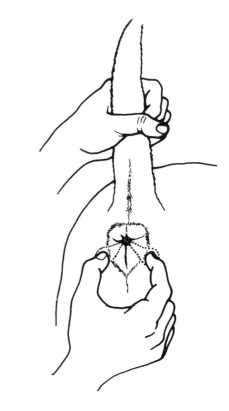

Figure 6-3
Press firmly to express the anal glands. Position of the glands is indicated by the dotted line.

become severely clogged, infection will set in and sacs may abscess. The only way to correct the abscess is to have the glands surgically removed.

Removing the accumulated fluid regularly will prevent impaction and will make your Beardie more confortable. Seize the tail with your left hand and encircle the anus from the bottom with your right hand. Press the anus firmly between your thumb and forefinger, expelling the vile-smelling mass. It may squirt some distance, so either do this outside or in an easily cleaned area, or cover the anus with a tissue or a piece of cotton. Repeating this procedure once a month is ample to keep the glands cleaned out, and, as stated earlier, the best time to check is just before a bath. Be sure to empty both glands.

Eye Care

Prolonged watering or irritation of the eyes is cause for concern, although it will probably occur for a few weeks as the puppy coat grows out and reaches a length where it gets into the eyes. You can help to avoid this by plucking the hair in the inner corner of the eyes. This problem corrects itself as the coat lengthens.

For mild irritation, a rinse made from one-fourth teaspoon salt in one-half cup water may be used, or you can buy a bottle of artificial tears for contact-lens wearers and use that as an eyewash. Severe irritation, mattering eyes, mild inflammation that does not clear up in a few days, or dilated pupils, haziness over the eye, or a foreign object in the eye signal a quick trip to your veterinarian. Don't put it off. And don't use old medication for a new eye problem. Drops or ointments for use in the eye are very specific to a particular condition and may cause serious injury if used to treat a different condition. Use medications only under the direction of your veterinarian. Avoid giving hepatitis vaccine to a dog with any eye irritation. It can create a severe reaction and possible blindness.

Beardie a la naturale!

Am Can. Ch. Classical Mystique, CD likes to sailboard. Courtesy Bridgette Nowak.

7 *Shaping Up*

THE HEALTHY BEARDIE

Optimum condition is essential in a show, working, or breeding Beardie, and it is important for the pet dog as well. Top condition is not achieved haphazardly but is the result of a skillfully planned and followed program. Conditioning is an ongoing project. The needs and condition of your Beardie will change from time to time during his life-span due to age, environment, stress, and other factors, so you will find it necessary to make adjustments in his diet and routine to compensate for these changes. Each Beardie is a little different. There are guidelines to help, but you will want to experiment a bit with your individual dog.

If you are to maintain your Beardie in glowing health and condition, you must first learn to recognize the signs of good health as well as the symptoms of illness or poor condition. Whether your dog lives in the house with you or in the kennel, be constantly alert to his condition and check him at least twice weekly. At first this will take conscious effort, but as you become familiar with your Beardie, the routine will become second nature.

Good health is dependent upon many factors—heredity, environment, diet, exercise, and grooming, to name a few. A healthy Beardie is bright and active with a happy, enthusiastic personality. His movements are effortless and smooth with no signs of stiffness or limping, and he does not tire easily. His coat appears glossy and unbroken, and beneath it you will find the skin smooth, pliable, and free from dandruff, scabs, red spots, or parasites.

A Bearded Collie in good condition carries just enough weight so that you can feel his ribs but cannot press a finger between them. Individual show Beardies may look better with just a bit more flesh, but they should never be fat. The muscles should be firm and supple, not soft and flabby. The flesh should fit the body firmly; loose, bouncing rolls of flesh are an indication of poor muscle tone

You can tell a great deal about your Beardie's health by observing the key areas—eyes, ears, and mouth. A Beardie's eyes may be the window to his soul, and they are also the first to clue you that he is not well. In a healthy Beardie, the eyes are clear, bright, expressive, and alert. The inside of the eyelids, as well as the third eyelid (the membrane at the inner corner between the upper and lower lids) are pink in color. (The third eyelid may have a dark pigment instead of a pink color.) Redness or swelling in these areas indicates a problem, and so do dull, cloudy eyes. The eyes should not water or contain mucus.

Lift your Beardie's ear leather and you will find the inside of the ear canal to be pale pink in color. It will be clearly visible if you have kept it free of hair (*see* Chapter 6). Bright pink or red ear membranes are abnormal. The ear should have only a small amount of brown wax. Large amounts of brown, orange, or foul-smelling wax are not normal.

The gums are also a vital key to good health. Become familiar with the normal color of your Beardie's gums and mouth. Normal gums are either pink or black, and they feel firm and fit tightly around the base of the teeth. Red, pale pink, yellowish, or white gums are abnormal. A red line along the gums, which appear to have shrunk away from the teeth, may indicate gum disease

During grooming, run your hands over your Beardie's body. You should find no lumps, swellings, or sores. Become familiar with your dog's respiration patterns both while at rest and after running. (Observe his usual sleeping, eating, bowel-movement, and urinating patterns.) Paying attention to these little details while he is well will enable you to notice quickly any abnormal behavior or appearance. You will detect an illness before it becomes serious and will be able to make minor adjustments in your dog's environment or conditioning program that will keep him in top shape at all times.

FEEDING

Your Beardie's diet is the greatest factor in achieving optimum condition and health. Therefore, you will want to choose a high-quality, properly balanced commercial ration. The best commercial dog-food manufacturers have conducted feeding trials and laboratory tests and will be happy to provide you with information on the results. Avoid brands that cannot or will not provide this information. Quality food contains minimum levels of carbohydrates, fats, and protein as well as minerals and vitamins essential to good canine nutrition.

In the United States, an excellent indication of quality is a statement on the label that the diet has been approved by the Association of American Feed Control Officials (AAFCO) protocol. An analysis of the ingredients in a particular food is not adequate because an element may be present but not in a form that the dog can digest and absorb. For example, chicken feathers are protein but are worthless as nutrition. Also, many nutrients, too numerous to itemize, are required. Toxic substances may be present in low-quality rations. Select a well-known manufacturer whose brand of dog food is recommended by your veterinarian and by other breeders. When you find a ration that maintains your Beardie in good condition, stay with it. Variety is not the "spice of life" when feeding your dog. In fact, changing his diet will often cause him to go off feed or have an upset stomach.

Types of Food

There are five basic types of diets. The first is the homemade diet. It *may* be nutritionally balanced, but because it rarely is, it can cause

"Is it dinnertime yet?"
Courtesy Artisan Beardies.

nutritional deficiencies, excesses, toxicities, and general imbalance

The second type, generally sold in grocery stores, pet shops, or feed stores, was referred to previously as "commercial" dog food, usually cereal-based. These brands are generally available in a maintenance ration but also may be obtained in a growth ration, which has a higher protein and energy content for growing puppies or lactating bitches.

The third type includes foods containing various drugs. These fairly recent products are usually available only through your vet or a specialty house. One type, called HRH, contains drugs to help control heartworms, roundworms, and hookworms. Another brand now being developed will contain a progesterone compound for birth control.

The fourth kind of diet is the prescription diet, especially formulated for use in the management of certain medical conditions and available only by prescription from a veterinarian.

The fifth type is the premium-food diet, usually based on chicken, beef, or lamb, and containing all of the essential elements, thus needing no additional supplementation of any kind except the possibility of oil for the coat. Most of these are sold only in feed or pet stores or by veterinarians. These rations are usually obtain-

able in formulations for maintenance, lactation, growth, and stress. They are highly concentrated and highly digestible, and feeding them will result in a lower stool volume.

Forms of Food

Three forms of dog food are available: dry, soft-moist, and canned.

Dry Food. Dry foods are cheaper, may be self-fed, and are abrasive enough to help prevent formation of tartar on the teeth. The disadvantage of this food is that it supplies a great deal of bulk. As a result, a Beardie under stress or with unusually high energy requirements may not eat enough to maintain correct weight. Also, dry food is sometimes deficient in the fatty acids, which aid in maintaining good coat and skin condition. This can be easily offset by adding one tablespoon of vegetable oil to each pound of dry food. Dry food loses its fatty acids to oxidation and becomes rancid if it is stored for more than six months (less than six months in extreme heat or humidity

Soft-Moist Food. Many brands of soft-moist (burger-type) foods are being marketed.

They are more expensive, cannot be self-fed, and contribute to tartar formation. They *may* contain a higher-quality protein or more energy per pound on a dry-matter basis. They definitely contain higher sugar and preservative percentages.

Canned Food. The advantages and disadvantages of canned food are similar to those of soft-moist food. Each can contains about 77 percent water, which means that more than three-fourths of the cost is for water. A dog must eat a much larger volume of canned food to obtain his daily nutritional requirements, and this makes canned food impractical for Bearded Collies.

Methods of Feeding

A dog may be either self-fed or individually fed. The only requirement for self-feeding is to leave food (dry food only) before your Beardie at all times. Self-feeding allows you more freedom to come and go, it is easy, and it requires no mixing, adjusting, or record-keeping. Each dog eats what he wants when he wants it. Self-feeding helps to discourage the eating of feces. The dog that likes to eat only small amounts at a time will often do best on self-feeding, but some dogs may overeat and get fat. Puppies that are self-fed may overeat, resulting in an overly rapid growth pattern and associated skeletal problems. A drawback to self-feeding is that the food can attract mice and insects, and even birds if fed outdoors.

A self-feeding program must be started slowly to discourage overeating. At first, feed the normal ration, then gradually increase the amount until some food is left at the end of each day. Self-feeding is not recommended for some Beardie puppies until they are at least six months of age. You may want to experiment to determine which of your dogs do best on self-feeding programs. If you have more than one Beardie, they all must do well on self-feeding unless they are kenneled separately.

If you feed your Beardies individually, any type of food may be given, and the amount of food and supplementation should be balanced for each dog. Puppies less than six months of age and lactating bitches should be fed at least twice daily. In fact, evidence suggests that two feedings per day are better than one for all dogs, although many breeders feed adult dogs only once daily. A big advantage to individual feeding is that you can tell immediately if a dog is going off feed.

You can teach your Beardie to clean up his bowl by placing him in an area where he can eat alone and undisturbed. Pick up his bowl in about fifteen minutes whether he has finished or not. He will soon learn to complete his meal in the allotted time. Once-a-day feeding can be either in the morning or the evening, whichever fits your schedule the best, but it should be at approximately the same time every day.

Whatever type of food and method of feeding you select, avoid oversupplementing with vitamins and minerals. Supplements, when fed improperly, can do more harm than good, so use them only under your veterinarian's guidance. Avoid giving table scraps, sweets, or bones to your Beardie. You'll only encourage obesity, begging, or finicky eating. Knuckle bones of beef may be parboiled to kill parasites and can be given occasionally but are very abrasive to the teeth. Do not give your Beardie pork, steak, chicken, or other small bones. Many dogs have died from a bone-punctured intestine.

How much should you feed? This is difficult to answer, because each Beardie has a slightly different metabolism. Your best gauge is your dog's weight and condition. A dog that is too thin or too fat is probably eating too little or too much, respectively. Generally an adult Beardie can be expected to consume about four cups of dry food per day.

Food Supplements

Many food additives and nutritional supplements are available, but they are generally unnecessary if your adult Beardie is being fed a high-quality ration. It is safer, cheaper, and easier to buy a good-quality, balanced ration than to supplement a low-quality food. Vitamins, minerals, and nutrients must be supplied in balanced ratios to be effective, otherwise they can cause problems. It is difficult to duplicate scientifically balanced diets with home methods.

Beardie puppies between two and six months of age exhibit an unusually fast growth rate, and they may need added calcium and phosphorus unless they are being fed a premium-quality food specifically formulated for growth. If you must add these elements, the safest way to do so is by adding one tablespoon of bone meal to the food each day. It is inexpensive and can be purchased from pet supply or health food stores.

Beardies living in a dry climate, or those fed a dry kibble, may need a coat supplement to furnish additional fatty acids. Many commercial formulas are on the market, or you may simply add corn, vegetable, safflower, peanut, or soy oil at the rate of one tablespoon per pound of dry food. Fats from meat other than bacon supply only empty calories instead of the needed fatty acids and should not be used.

CONDITIONING THROUGH EXERCISE

Your conditioning program cannot be complete without planned exercise. The amount of exercise that your Beardie gets has as much control over his weight and bloom as does his diet. A fat, soft Beardie needs more exercise, perhaps accompanied by a more restricted diet. A thin or overmuscled dog usually needs less exercise along with, perhaps, a diet higher in calories. Exercise often improves appetite, and a thin dog that is not eating properly may be induced to eat more by increasing his activity.

Often, neither the kennel dog nor the house pet gets the right type of exercise. Both should have at least one hour per day of romping in a large yard or exercise area where they can move freely. The show or working Beardie needs additional exercise, and this is best achieved through road work. Road work means trotting your Beardie for a structured period each day, usually on a leash behind a bicycle or automobile, until he develops his maximum potential gait and endurance. With consistent road work, the Beardie that moves sloppily will tighten up, the good-moving dog will develop a gait that is effortless, smooth, and extended, and the tight dog will begin to move more freely. You can't correct real unsoundness through road work, but you can make the most of what your Beardie is capable of doing.

Adult Beardies should be initiated at about one-half mile per day, moving at a comfortable trotting speed on a loose leash. Do not allow your dog to gallop or pace—this develops entirely different muscles. The best surface for road work is dirt or cut grass. If you have only gravel or concrete surfaces, you will have to work shorter distances and check frequently for signs of sore pads or lameness. The surface should be level or slightly uphill. Never trot a dog downhill—it breaks down pasterns and shoulders.

Never work your Beardie until he is exhausted, stiff, or lame. If this occurs at any point, rest him for a day or two, then shorten the distance worked until it is comfortable for him. By the end of the first week, most Beardies will be ready to proceed to trotting one mile per day. Week by week, gradually lengthen the distance until your dog is easily trotting two or three miles daily.

After your dog has reached his maximum distance, it will take at least a month of consistent, daily road work for him to approach peak performance. After this point you can maintain optimum performance by working him only two or three times weekly. If you wish your dog to be at his best for show season, start his workouts about three months prior to the first show.

Puppies may be started on road work at about six months of age, but they should be worked much shorter distances and should progress more slowly from one distance to the next.

Never tie a Beardie behind a car. Instead, have someone drive while you sit on the tailgate

Four-month-old puppies exercise themselves by playing. Courtesy Michele Ritter.

of a station wagon and lead the dog (don't position him where he must breathe the exhaust fumes). Or, still better for you, ride a bicycle. You can buy a unit that attaches to your bicycle and holds the dog away from the wheels and that also has a spring to absorb any shock if the dog pulls away. A good trotting speed for an adult Beardie averages seven to eight miles per hour.

If you can't manage either of these methods, or if you have several dogs to work, treadmills are available for dogs. These have the advantage of being usable in any weather, although they don't give *you* any exercise. One dedicated Beardie owner set up a stationary bicycle beside the treadmill and pedaled while his dog trotted.

CARING FOR THE OLDER BEARDIE

Without your hardly noticing it, your Beardie will one day move a little slower and sleep a little longer. His body processes will slow, his resistance will be lower, and his digestion, sight, and hearing will not be as good as they once

were. But he will still be an important member of your family and can be depended upon to assist in training younger dogs. He will add an air of permanency and dignity to your household. He will be living proof of your healthy line of Beardies and will probably be a super-salesman besides.

The older Beardie requires little in additional care: a warmer, drier place to sleep; encouragement to exercise; and perhaps a special diet lower in protein to help keep his weight down and not overstress his kidneys. Loss of teeth may make food difficult to chew, so switch to a softer food and have his teeth cleaned regularly.

The older dog is often subject to cysts (which sometimes look like pimples on the skin), various infections, deafness, or blindness. In familiar surroundings, you may never know that your dog is blind, but he will become frightened and bump into things when taken to a different environment. A blind dog can be taught to respond to sound vibrations, and a deaf dog can respond to hand signals and still live a reasonably happy, comfortable life.

When the day comes that your Beardie can no longer lead a meaningful existence, or when his days are filled with suffering, you should consider ending his misery through euthanasia. No one wants to give up a friend, but it is often the best way for him. Your veterinarian will inject an overdose of anesthetic, and your Beardie will drift into a peaceful, permanent sleep. The process takes only a few seconds; there is no pain or fright, and no prolonged suffering.

Beardies enjoy sharing all aspects of your life. Courtesy Brigette Nowak.

Courtesy Diane and Dorine Wynen.

Willowmead Summer Magic takes a bow. Courtesy Collavechio.

8 *In Sickness and In Health*

You can protect your pet from many canine diseases by providing yearly vaccinations and preventive care. In addition, cleanliness and maintenance of a parasite-free environment will assure that your Beardie stays healthy. You are fortunate to have chosen a breed with relatively few hereditary problems or tendencies to illness. Yet, every dog owner at some point will be called upon to administer first aid or give medication for a minor illness. You will want to familiarize yourself with symptoms of illness, antidotes for poisons, and medical techniques so that you will be prepared.

IMMUNIZATIONS

Beardie puppies usually get their first immunization shot at five to seven weeks of age. Not all veterinarians agree on the schedule for vaccinating puppies, so it is best to follow your own veterinarian's advice. Puppies receive antibodies from their mother's milk, and immunization will not take effect until all of this maternal immunity has been lost. This can occur anywhere between six and sixteen weeks of age; therefore, the puppy should be protected from exposure to disease during his first three months, and the final immunization is given when he is three to four months old. Thereafter, yearly boosters are required. When you buy a puppy, the breeder should give you a record of the type and pharmaceutical of the shots and when they were given.

Rabies vaccinations are required by law and are given when a puppy is three to six months old. The same state laws also regulate the frequency of booster vaccinations. The American Veterinary Association recommends a booster vaccination for modified live-virus rabies one year after the initial shot, then boosters every one to three years. A certificate of rabies vaccination will be required when you apply for a city or county dog license or a health certificate for interstate shipping. Many localities require yearly boosters.

PARASITES

Parasites are dependent at some point in their life cycle on a host—your dog. They are common in almost any area of the world, and, while they generally do not represent a serious problem, they should be eliminated. They are often the cause of poor overall condition, thinness, dull, dry coats, and lack of vigor.

All parasites complete a life cycle, only part of which affects your dog. This cycle must be considered or you will continue to have the problem even after you have treated your dog.

Internal Parasites

The most common internal parasites are roundworms, tapeworms, hookworms, whipworms, and giardia, all of which live in the dog's intestine. You may or may not see the worms or their symptoms. Microscopic diagnosis by a veterinarian is necessary. You will want to have your puppy checked several times the first year and every year thereafter by taking a small amount of fresh stool for an examination.

Roundworms or Ascarids

These white, cylindrical worms are the most common type seen in puppies. Puppies can be born with roundworms, or they can pick up the eggs from contaminated surfaces after birth.

Keep your Beardie puppy a picture of health by preventing disease and parasites.
Am. Can. Ch. Classical's Silver Cloud.
Courtesy Classical Kennels.

Either way, it is safe to assume that almost every puppy will be infected with these worms.

Adult roundworms live in the small intestine, where they absorb nutrients from the digestive juices. The worms produce eggs that pass in the stool. The eggs become larvae, are ingested by either the same individual or another dog, and develop into worms to complete the cycle. Some of the larvae will not complete the cycle but will migrate into the lungs or other tissue to remain in a resting stage. When a bitch becomes pregnant, these resting larvae migrate into the fetus.

Beardies with roundworm infections may appear thin and potbellied. They may have dull coats or diarrhea, or they may vomit or cough. In young puppies, a heavy infection may cause death, but in adult dogs, the worms do not generally cause a serious illness. Roundworms are easily eliminated with a drug called piperazine.

It is safe and can be obtained from your vet or from a pet-supply store. It can be given to puppies as young as two weeks of age. The treatment should be repeated in two weeks and again in a month to make sure that all of the mature worms are killed.

The biggest problem with roundworms is that the eggs can remain alive and infective in the soil for months. Cleanliness is important. Remove the stool daily and control rodents, which serve as an intermediate host to the larvae. Treat the soil with salt or borax (*see* Chapter 5).

Tapeworms

This parasite attaches to the intestinal wall with suckers. The tapeworm's body is composed of a series of reproductive segments that look somewhat like grains of rice. They may sometimes be seen clinging to the hair or skin around the anus, or on the stool. The adult tapeworm produces eggs that pass in the feces and are eaten by an intermediate host, such as a rodent, louse, flea, or rabbit. The dog then eats the intermediate host containing the effective stage of the tapeworm, and the worm completes its life cycle by developing in the dog's intestine.

Tapeworms may cause digestive problems, weight loss, or poor condition. Avoid using tapeworm medication available in drug or pet stores, because it generally is ineffective and can be dangerous. Your vet can provide a safe, effective dewormer. Again, cleanliness and elimination of intermediate hosts, especially fleas, are required to prevent reinfection.

Hookworms

Hookworms are small worms that suck blood directly from the wall of the small intestine. They are one of the more tenacious and more damaging parasites. Dogs become infested by ingesting the larvae from the ground or by having their skin or pads penetrated by the infective larvae. Puppies are often infected before birth by the migrating larvae.

Symptoms include weakness, diarrhea, anemia, and blood in the stool. The stool is black and looks like tar with a distinctive odor. Heavily infected puppies may die before the worms are detected. Treatment must be administered quickly by a veterinarian, and blood transfusions may be necessary. All hookworm medications can be dangerous and should be used under the direction of your veterinarian. Do not use over-the-counter medications sold for these worms, because they can cause severe side effects.

Whipworms

These parasites live in the large intestine and may cause diarrhea or weight loss. They can be detected only by microscopic examination and require a specific wormer that your veterinarian can prescribe.

Heartworms

Heartworm disease is a very serious problem. The adult heartworms live in the right atrium and ventricle of the heart. The mature worms produce larvae called microfilaria, which circulate in the blood. When a mosquito bites an infected dog, that insect becomes the intermediate host for the microfilaria, which can be passed on when another dog is bitten. Once found mainly in the southern states, heartworm disease is now found throughout the United States

Infected dogs tire easily, cough, have difficulty breathing, and are generally in poor condition. Signs of heart failure may occur. However, heartworm may be present for some time before symptoms appear. Treatment can be long and difficult, and hospitalization is often required.

Fortunately, there is a very effective method of prevention. Two types of medication are available that will kill microfilaria before they mature into adult worms. Both medications come in pill form, and one type is given daily, the other once a month. It is necessary for a veterinarian to do a blood test before prescribing heartworm pills.

Protozoa

Protozoa are tiny, one-celled parasites that live in the intestines. Stools of an infected dog can be thin and watery, dark and loose, or covered in a thick mucus. A persistent diarrhea can occur that is resistant to the usual antidiarrheal drugs but that does not cause vomiting or lethargy. A protozoan infection can be very difficult to diagnose, because it requires immediate examination of fresh fecal matter and is easily missed unless looked for specifically.

Giardia. This parasite absorbs carbohydrates directly from the host. It was once thought to be rare but is found increasingly throughout the world. It is spread through contact with fecal matter, often in water in areas inhabited by wild animals. Dogs can be treated with drugs, or a mild infection can be left to run its course. Adult dogs build up a resistance to it, but once infected, they can carry encysted eggs that can become infective in a new host.

Coccidia. Coccidia is more common in puppies than in adult dogs. It is often characterized by yellow stools that have a distinctive, foul odor. Coccidia is found most frequently in filthy conditions, although a bitch that has been infected can carry it encapsulated in muscle tissue and this, in turn, can infect her puppies. It will usually run its course in a week or so, but young puppies can easily become dehydrated and may require treatment.

External Parasites

Fleas. Fleas are by far the most common external parasite found on dogs, cats, and other animals. The two kinds most often found on dogs are the fairly large, brown dog fleas and the much smaller, shiny black sand fleas. Fleas suck blood and therefore can significantly weaken the host as well as spread disease. Fleas deposit eggs about the size and color of a grain of salt on their host. The eggs drop off into bedding, into cracks in the soil or in buildings, into carpets, etc. In about two weeks, the eggs hatch into larvae, which then develop into adult fleas.

To control the parasites, you must eliminate them on your dog through the use of medicated shampoo or insecticide powders, then thoroughly clean all bedding and housing or kennel facilities. You may want to fumigate your house or kennel, or spray with lindane or malathion. Discard old bedding. A new pill administered once a month as a preventative has recently been released.

Lice. Lice are small, pale-colored, blood-sucking insects that are far less common than fleas. They are generally found only in extremely dirty conditions or around poultry facilities. They can be treated by the same methods used against fleas. Because lice die quickly once removed from their host, it is not necessary to treat the bedding.

Ticks. Ticks are a problem in some areas of the country. There are many different species, all of which attach themselves to the dog's flesh and engorge themselves with the blood of their host. They can cause anemia, weakness, or paralysis.

If your dog has only one or two, you can remove them by hand. Apply a little rubbing alcohol to the tick, causing it to loosen, then grasp the insect firmly as close to the dog's skin as possible and slowly pull the tick off. You can then burn it with a match.

If ticks are a constant problem, or your dog has picked up a number of them, purchase a good commercial tick and flea dip and spray, or fumigate bedding and kennel facilities. You may have to repeat the spraying several times before all ticks are killed.

Deer ticks that carry Lyme Disease are an increasing problem in many areas of the country. Lyme Disease is difficult to diagnose, because it mimics other conditions. Limping or arthritic symptoms are often the first signs. A vaccine is currently available but is not yet approved in all states, so check with your veterinarian.

WHEN YOUR BEARDIE IS NOT FEELING WELL

Once you have learned to observe the signs of good health in your dog and have become familiar with his habits and behavior, it will be easy to determine when he is ill. Any change in behavior or appetite can be a clue. He may be restless, depressed, or ill-tempered, or he may whine. His eyes may appear dull and uninterested, or they may water. He may vomit, have diarrhea, shiver, or appear to be uncomfortable. He may show signs of stiffness, or lameness, or he may urinate frequently. A fever is a definite indication of illness.

Any dog may have an off day, so don't panic at first. Just be observant. Take your Beardie's rectal temperature using any human rectal thermometer inserted about half its length. The normal temperature for most canines is 101.5 degrees, but be aware (and also inform your vet) that it is often normal for a Beardie to have a temperature of 102.0 or even 102.5. It will be highest in the afternoon or evening. Check your dog's temperature several different times while he is healthy to determine what is normal for him.

If your dog appears to behave abnormally for more than one day, or if acute symptoms or a high fever are present, take him to your veterinarian for a checkup, or call for advice. It is important for every dog owner to locate within close proximity a good veterinarian and establish a good relationship with him or her.

Giving Medication

With a little practice, you can give your Beardie a pill easily and quickly. To force your dog's mouth open, grasp his muzzle with your hand over his foreface and let your fingers press his upper lips over the tips of his upper teeth. Tilt his head upward slightly to encourage swallowing. With your other hand, place the pill far back in the center of the base of the tongue. Quickly remove your hand and close your dog's mouth, holding it closed until you feel him swallow. Rubbing the throat will sometimes encourage swallowing. If the pill is particularly large or dry, buttering it will help.

Liquid medication may be given from a spoon, but drawing it into a large syringe (minus a needle!), an eyedropper, or a kitchen

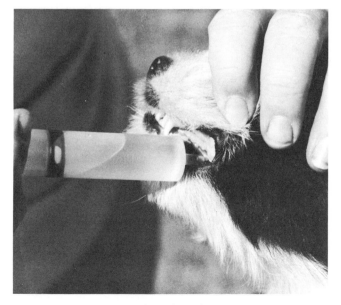

Giving liquid medication.

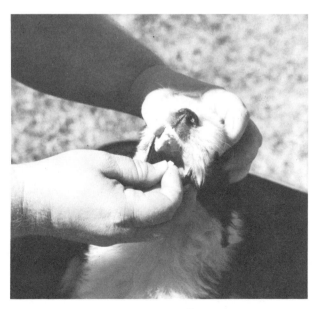

Giving a pill.

baster makes it easier to administer. Pull the corner of the lower lip outward and upward with one hand, forming a pocket. Keeping your Beardie's head tilted slightly upward, slowly pour the liquid into the lip pocket. Allow your dog to swallow as the liquid is given, but prevent him from shaking or lowering his head.

It is important when giving medications to administer the exact quantity specified. Pills should not be crushed into the food, because you can never be sure that they are being swallowed entirely.

Supplies

Every dog owner should have a medicine chest that includes the following: a rectal thermometer, a good liquid antiseptic, soap, cotton swabs, peroxide, gauze pads and a gauze bandage wrap, alcohol, clean towels, a blunt-nosed scissors for clipping around wounds, etc., styptic powder or silver nitrate to control bleeding of small wounds or bites, an old nylon stocking for use as a muzzle, Kaopectate, Milk of Magnesia tablets, a good antiseptic wound spray, a general purpose flea and tick dip or shampoo, Panolog dressing, Dramamine™, artificial tears for eyes, activated charcoal and a product such as Bitter Apple to prevent chewing.

Some Common Diseases and Problems

Arthritis. Properly called osteoarthritis, this is a disease in which the joints are affected by excess bone growth, resulting in pain and lameness. It can occur in young dogs due to trauma affecting a joint or from congenital joint defects. It more commonly occurs with aging.

Treatment is only symptomatic; there is no way to arrest the development of arthritis. Keep the arthritic Beardie warm and dry, and limit, but do not discontinue, exercise. Do not allow the dog to become overweight. Your vet may prescribe aspirin or Tylenol if the pain is severe, or in more advanced cases may suggest corticosteroids.

Conversion Table

16 drops = 1 cc = ¼ teaspoon
5 cc = 1 teaspoon
15 cc = 1 tablespoon = ½ ounce
30 cc = 2 tablespoons = 1 ounce
8 ounces = 1 cup
4 cups = 1 quart = 1 liter

Constipation. Constipation commonly occurs from lack of bulk in the diet but also may be caused by overlong confinement (especially while traveling), internal parasites, tumors, abscessed anal sacs, or old age. One day without a bowel movement is no cause for concern.

A mild change in diet or adding water to the food may help. Two tablespoons of Milk of Magnesia or one of the human laxatives designed to provide bulk may be given, or try a human rectal suppository.

Dermatitis. There are many kinds of dermatitis, or inflammation of the skin—some caused by allergies, some by contact with irritants, and some by infection. The symptoms are similar: red skin accompanied by hair loss in the area, and possibly bumps, scabs, dandruff-like scales, or oozing areas. The skin may feel hot to the touch.

Severe dermatitis requires veterinary attention. You may try treating small areas by bathing your dog frequently and rinsing him with one capful of Alpha-Keri per quart of water. Apply Furaspor or some other type of soothing, drying ointment to the area.

Diarrhea. Diarrhea may indicate a more serious disease or infection, or it may be the result of overeating, a change in diet, overexcitement, or the presence of parasites. The best initial treatment is to withhold food for twelve to twenty-four hours, then limit your dog to a light, bland diet containing broth, cooked eggs, cottage cheese, or rice for several days. Kaopectate can be given every four hours (two teaspoonfuls per ten pounds of weight).

Severe diarrhea, diarrhea accompanied by vomiting, or bloody diarrhea signals a trip to your veterinarian. Unchecked diarrhea causes dehydration, which can occur especially rapidly in puppies. Beware of administering some of the commercial products sold by pet-supply catalogs. They can be quite strong and possibly dangerous.

Distemper. Distemper is a highly contagious, infectious disease. The germs are airborne, so direct contact with an infected animal is not required. Distemper virus is everywhere; you can even carry the germs into your home on shoes or clothing. For this reason, and because the disease is generally fatal, every dog should be immunized with yearly boosters throughout his life

Symptoms are erratic. Often, the first signs include fever, listlessness, lack of appetite, stiffness, or vomiting. Later, the dog will probably develop diarrhea, nasal discharge, and coughing. Eventually, the nervous system becomes damaged.

Ear Inflammation. If your Beardie begins shaking his head and scratching at his ears, he may have an ear infection. The insides of the ear may be red or swollen, have large amounts of waxy discharge, or emit a strong odor. First, remove any excess hair from the ear canal by plucking. Try cleaning the ear with a cotton swab dipped in 70 percent isopropyl alcohol. Then place several drops of alcohol into the ear and massage the base of the ear to spread the medication. Severe or continued ear infectionsshould be treated by a veterinarian.

Ear Mites. These parasites are common in some parts of the country. They cause discomfort and scratching, accompanied by profuse amounts of dark reddish-brown to gray wax. If you live in an area where ear mites are common, your vet can give you drops containing lindane, rotenone, or some other insecticide. Clean the ear with a cotton swab dipped in isopropyl alcohol. You may be able to see the small mites. Drop the insecticide into the ears according to instructions.

Eye Irritations and Inflammations. Eyes are very delicate organs, and even the slightest irritation should not be ignored. Often, dust, pollen, or a foreign object or allergy will cause tearing or mild inflammation. Wash the eye area with a cotton swab dipped in a saltwater solution (one teaspoon salt per one cup water), or use artificial tears sold for humans. If the irritation continues, see your vet. Never use anything in the eye that is not specifically designed for ophthalmic use, and never use eye drugs prescribed for one problem to treat another case. Ophthalmic drugs are very specific; using the wrong one could cause blindness.

Conjunctivitis, or inflammation of the third eyelid, is a fairly common problem. The membrane appears red and swollen. Treatment with antibiotics is necessary.

Enteritis. Enteritis is acute, hemorrhagic diarrhea accompanied by cramping of the stomach, gas, and vomiting. The onset is sudden. Give your dog two tablespoons of Kaopectate to quiet his stomach and rush him to the vet. Causes of enteritis are varied, but sudden death can result unless treatment is begun immediately.

Heart Disease. There are a number of different heart problems that affect dogs, more commonly older dogs. All conditions generally progress from mild stages to more serious forms. Heart failure usually can be treated and controlled if discovered early. A Beardie suffering from heart disease may tire more easily. You may notice him coughing in the morning or evening, or after exertion. He may gag up mucus. In severe cases, you may notice an unusual arrhythmia, or murmur, in the heartbeat, or your dog may have difficulty breathing. Treatment for heart disease often involves regulation of the diet as well as administration of drugs.

Infectious Canine Hepatitis. Canine hepatitis is not the same as human hepatitis, although it is similar in that the disease primarily affects the liver. It is an acute viral disease characterized by high fever, bloody diarrhea, abdominal pain, and vomiting. Dogs may exhibit an intolerance for light, and occasionally a blue film will form over the cornea of the eye. This condition is known as "blue eye" and can occur from mild forms of the disease, or rarely, from a reaction to the vaccine. Hepatitis vaccine should never be given to a dog with an eye ulceration, because an extreme reaction and possible blindness may result

There is no cure for the disease. Hospitalization is required, but only the symptoms can be treated. You can protect your Beardie with vaccinations administered yearly in conjunction with distemper vaccine.

Kennel Cough. Tracheobronchitis, known as "kennel cough" because it occurs frequently in kennels, at shows, or anyplace where large numbers of dogs come together, is one of the most contagious of canine diseases. It is characterized by a dry, hacking cough or deep, harsh coughing often accompanied by gagging. The Beardie's appetite will remain good, and he will have no fever or other symptoms. Like a cold, kennel cough must run its course, and most dogs will recover with or without medication in two to six weeks if they are kept warm and relatively quiet. Occasionally, a stubborn case will hang on for several months. Over-the-counter cough suppressants marketed for humans may be given to mask the symptoms, and your veterinarian can prescribe broad-spectrum antibiotics.

A vaccine can immunize your Beardie against some forms of kennel cough. The immunization can be given separately or combined with the DHL vaccine. Be sure to request it if you have a number of dogs or plan to travel or show your Beardie.

Kidney and Bladder Infections. The most common problems affecting the urinary system are interstitial nephritis in the kidneys, or cystitis (bladder infection).

Nephritis is common in older dogs, but it can occur in conjunction with infectious diseases or be caused by the ingestion of poisons. An affected Beardie generally runs a fever, arches his back in pain, drinks increased amounts of water, vomits, and has strong body or breath odors. A urinalysis is required for diagnosis, and hospitalization may be required. Prompt treatment will usually prevent kidney damage in acute cases. Chronic nephritis is controlled by diet and medication.

Cystitis is generally caused by a bacterial infection in the bladder. Symptoms include frequent urination, cloudy or blood-tinged urine, and straining. Females may have a vaginal discharge and may lick themselves excessively. Treatment with antibiotics will be required for several weeks, and the dog should have plenty of water.

If you think that your Beardie has a kidney or bladder problem, collect a urine sample within an hour before you leave, and take it to your vet. Take your Beardie out on the leash and collect about one-fourth cup of urine in a clean container.

Leptospirosis. Leptospirosis is the third kind of infectious disease against which dogs are immunized, and it is the only one that is contagious to humans.

The disease primarily affects the kidneys, causing kidney failure. Germs are spread in the contaminated urine from affected dogs, rodents, or cattle. Rat- or mouse-contaminated foods are a prime source. The bacteria can enter a dog's system orally, through the skin, or during intercourse.

Symptoms include depression, loss of appetite, vomiting, fever, and constipation followed by diarrhea. The dog may be stiff and reluctant to move, often walking in a hunched-up posture with short, choppy steps. Occasionally, the infection is so slight that it is hardly noticeable; in other cases, it may cause death. Recovered animals may carry the germs for months afterward.

Vaccination will protect your Beardie from leptospirosis. The disease is more prevalent in some parts of the country than in others, and the vaccine, usually administered as part of the DHL package, may not be given routinely. Ask your vet for recommendations, and be sure to inform him or her if you plan to travel or ship your dog for breeding. The immunity is shorter-lived than other vaccines, and boosters every six months are required in high-risk areas.

Tonsillitis. If you open your Beardie's mouth wide, you can probably see his tonsils, which lie in a pocket on either side of the throat just behind the soft palate. Occasionally, they may become infected and may appear red and swollen. Your dog may refuse to eat or may have difficulty eating, or he may gag or vomit or have a slight fever. Tonsillitis is often caused by rapid changes in temperature, such as when a house dog is left in the cold too long, or a kennel dog is switched between the house and an unheated kennel in cold weather. Antibiotics are generally effective in clearing up the infection, but recurrent infections may lead to surgical removal of the tonsils.

Tumors. Older dogs are especially prone to abnormal tissue growths or tumors. Tumors may occur internally or on the outside of the body, commonly in the stomach or around the mammary glands of females. Tumors of the oil-producing glands are called sebaceous cysts. These are usually small, light-colored growths that somewhat resemble pimples. They may appear wart-like. They are usually benign and need no treatment but can be surgically removed if they become too large.

Vaginitis. Inflammation of the vagina is common in bitches. Young bitches may develop a type of vaginitis prior to their first heat. The condition is characterized by a mild irritation and discharge at the vulva, accompanied by an unusual attractiveness to male dogs. This form of vaginitis needs no treatment and will disappear with the first heat season.

Older bitches may exhibit a sticky yellowish, greenish, or gray discharge that will cause them to lick the vulva excessively. The mucous membranes may be red or red-spotted. The symptoms may be accompanied by a bladder infection and should be watched carefully. Otherwise, a more serious uterine condition, such as metritis or pyometra, may develop. Vaginitis can be treated successfully with antibiotics.

Vomiting. Your dog will often vomit when nothing is really wrong other than an upset stomach or the fact that he ate something that he shouldn't have eaten. He may first vomit food, followed by a frothy clear or yellow fluid. If he vomits only once or twice and has no fever, pain, or other symptoms of illness, don't worry. Just withhold food for about twelve hours, then feed him lightly with soft, bland food for the next day. Don't offer large amounts of water. You can often soothe your dog's stomach by giving Maalox or Mylanta (one teaspoon per twenty pounds of weight).

Vomiting from car sickness usually ends shortly after movement has stopped. You can sometimes prevent this discomfort by giving Dramamine™ about one-half hour before leaving

Severe vomiting, vomiting of blood, or vomiting accompanied by illness or depression should be treated immediately by a veterinarian. Your Beardie cannot talk, and by the time symptoms are observed, the illness may be fairly well progressed.

FIRST AID

Applied quickly and correctly, good first-aid measures can save your Beardie's life. Use *them only as a temporary emergency treatment to maintain the life of your dog until professional medical help is obtained*

What Constitutes an Emergency

Severe (life-threatening)
Respiratory failure
Cardiac arrest

Massive hemorrhage
Multiple, deep lacerations
Anaphylaxis (reaction to drug or
    immunization)
Penetrating wounds of the thorax
    or abdomen
Coma and loss of consciousness
Spinal fractures
Rapid-acting poisons
Massive musculoskeletal injuries
Acute overwhelming bacteremia and toxemia
Continual convulsions (no letup)

Severe
Multiple, deep lacerations
Skull and spinal injuries
Thoracic trauma without respiratory
    problems
Multiple pelvic or long-bone fractures

Moderate
Simple fractures of long bones, ribs, and
    pelvis
Luxations and ligament rupture
Deep lacerations and abrasions
Bacterial and viral infection with no
    depression

Minor
Cuts, wounds, scrapes of minor nature.

Transporting an Injured Beardie

Unless broken bones are obvious, an injured
dog may be carried by placing one arm under
his body, supporting his chest with your hand,
and cradling his body on your forearm. Steady
his head with your free hand.

A badly injured dog must be placed gently on
a solid board stretcher. Lacking anything solid,
you can improvise by placing two sticks through
the arms of a jacket or shirt to form a sling. Dis-
turb the dog's position as little as possible.

Figure 8-1
*Right: Transport an injured dog
on a sling made from a blanket or jacket.*

Applying a Muzzle

A Beardie that is in pain or shock may bite at
anyone who tries to handle him. To prevent
this, fashion a muzzle in the following manner:
tie the mouth shut with a piece of cloth or old
nylon stocking, making two additional wraps
around the muzzle with a hard knot under the
chin. Bring the two ends of the material behind
the ears and tie in a bow.

A properly applied muzzle.

Checking the Pulse

The normal heart rate of a Beardie is 90 to 100 beats per minute. You can feel your Beardie's pulse by locating the femoral artery. Place your index finger inside the hind leg as closely against the body as possible. You can also feel the pulse by placing your fingers over the heart itself.

Artificial Respiration

If you find your Beardie unconscious and not breathing, but with a heartbeat still audible, you may be able to revive him with artificial respiration.

Place the dog on his right side with his head and neck extended so that the windpipe makes a straight line. Pull the tongue forward and outward. With the heels of your hands, press the chest moderately hard just behind the shoulder blade, forcing air from the lungs. Relax the pressure, count to five, and repeat. The rhythm must be smooth and regular. Continue until your dog is breathing at his normal rate (about

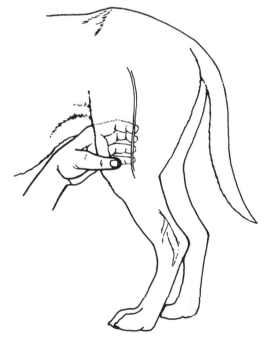

Figure 8-2
Hold your fingers over the dog's femoral artery and count the number of beats in six seconds. Multiply by ten to get beats per minute.

fifteen to twenty times per minute) without assistance. Then treat for shock.

You can also administer artificial respiration by placing your lips over your dog's mouth and nostrils, cupping your hands over them like a cone, and forcing air into his lungs.

Treating for Shock

A dog in shock appears depressed and has rapid heart and respiration rates, a rapid, weak pulse, and pale mucous membranes. He may shiver and feel cold to the touch. Breathing is slow, and the eyes are often glazed.

A dog in shock needs emergency veterinary treatment immediately. Wrap him in a towel or blanket for warmth, and if you are far from professional help, a tablespoon of whiskey may help revive him. Do not give water.

External Heart Massage

If your dog's heart has stopped, combine artificial respiration with external heart massage.¡

1. With the dog on his back, legs in the air, place the palms of your hands on his sternum, with your fingers on one side of the chest and your thumb on the other side.
2. Alternately compress and release the chest Compress the chest strongly between your thumb and fingers, pushing the ribs together. At the same time, press the sternum downward toward the spine. Release the pressure suddenly
3. Repeat the compression at the rate of seventy times per minute until the heart starts beating again. A dog can live about three minutes after the heart stops.

First Aid for Specific Conditions

Bee Stings. Apply an ice cube to the area and give your Beardie an aspirin tablet. If an allergic reaction sets in, consult your vet. Normally, the swelling will go down in forty-eight hours or less.

Bleeding. Cover the wound with sterile gauze and apply a pressure bandage by wrapping the injury tightly. Use a tourniquet between an arterial injury and the heart *only* if a pressure bandage will not control the bleeding. Tourniquets must be loosened every ten minutes.

Broken Nails. Apply a styptic powder or use powdered alum to stop the bleeding. Smooth the nail with a coarse file after bleeding has stopped.

Bruises. If the injury is recent and swelling has not yet begun, apply a cold compress. If the injury is swollen, apply a hot compress.

Burns. Run cold water over the area or apply an ice pack for about twenty minutes. Do not apply ointments of any kind. If a burn is serious, take your Beardie to the veterinary hospital immediately.

Cactus or Porcupine Quills. Remove them with tweezers or pliers. Treat with an antiseptic spray.

Cuts and Wounds. Wash with a 3-percent solution of hydrogen peroxide. You may pour the peroxide directly into the wound, use a cotton swab, or flush the solution into the wound with a syringe or baster. Repeat this procedure twice daily. Clip the hair around the wound to avoid irritation. Large tears or wounds will require sutures.

Dog Bites. Wash a dog bite with peroxide and treat with a topical antiseptic ointment. Deep puncture wounds or tears will need suturing.

Drowning. Hold your Beardie upside-down by his legs until water is drained from his lungs, then administer artificial respiration if needed. Keep your dog warm and rub his body vigorously. You may be able to revive an unconscious dog with spirits of ammonia held under his nostrils.

Frostbite or Chilling. Warm your dog slowly by wrapping him in warm towels. A puppy may be placed inside your coat. Apply tepid water to frozen feet, gradually increasing the temperature to 100 degrees. Do not apply dry heat. Give a tablespoon of whiskey as a stimulant.

Fractures. Move your dog as little as possible. Place him on a board or stretcher and take him to the veterinary hospital as soon as possible. Compound fractures, where bone has punctured the skin, require immediate attention. Other fractures that are not accompanied by shock can be treated within the day. Do not try to apply splints or bandages.

Heat Stroke. An overheated dog will pant, will have an increased pulse rate, and will appear anxious with a staring expression. He may vomit, or he may become unconscious. Immerse the dog in cold water, or if this is impossible, spray him with the garden hose. Massage the skin and legs to encourage circulation, and place ice cubes on his mouth and nose. Do not give stimulants or water. Immediate veterinary attention is needed.

Puncture Wounds. Remove small objects carefully and apply a pressure bandage. If the object is large or has punctured the eye or abdomen, let a veterinarian remove it.

Skunk Odor. Bathe your Beardie in tomato juice, followed by soap and water. Wash his eyes with a mild salt solution. If you cannot bathe him, you can make him a little more acceptable by rubbing him with a damp sponge sprinkled with baking soda. Commercial products are available for removing skunk odor.

Snakebites. Keep your dog immobilized as much as possible, with the wound at the same level as the heart. Use a snakebite kit or make a sharp cut at the wound to induce bleeding. If the bite is on a leg, apply a tourniquet loose enough to slip one finger underneath it, and leave it on the dog until you reach a vet. Get your Beardie to the veterinarian as soon as possible.

Swallowing a Foreign Object. Feed bread or other soft food that will wrap itself around the object. Check with your vet regarding further treatment.

Poisoning. Identifying the poison is of utmost importance. *Call a veterinarian.* If you *cannot* get a vet and you know what the poisonous material was, administer the antidote and then drive your dog to the clinic. *Do not treat for poisoning unless you are sure what material was ingested.* You can induce vomiting by giving one ounce peroxide in one ounce of water. Do not induce vomiting if the poison was corrosive.

If the poison was a contact poison, always wash the contact area with large amounts of water. If your dog goes into convulsions, try to keep him from injuring himself by muzzling him and holding him as still as possible until you get to the vet.

Some common household poisons include the following:

Alkalis: Household drain cleaner is the most common of this type. It causes profuse salivation, nausea, and sometimes vomiting. Give a neutralizing acid such as vinegar or lemon juice—two or three tablespoons should be enough.

Aniline dyes: Found in shoe polish, crayons, and other household dyes. The lip and oral membranes may turn brown, breathing is labored, and the dog is listless. Induce vomiting with peroxide and give coffee as a stimulant.

Aspirin: Too much aspirin will cause weakness, rapid breathing, stomach pain, and sometimes collapse. Induce vomiting. Then give the dog sodium bicarbonate (baking soda) in water

Bleaches: Cause a general upset stomach. Induce vomiting. Then give the dog an egg white or a little olive oil.

Cleaning fluids: Either inhaling the fumes or ingesting the substance may cause poisoning.

For inhalation poisoning, give artificial respiration if needed and move your dog to a well-ventilated area. Wash his eyes with water. If the fluid was swallowed, induce vomiting, and give a dose of olive oil. Be careful that the oil does not go down the windpipe and choke your dog.

Cyanide or phosphorus: Found in some rat poisons. These are fast-acting poisons and cause pain, convulsions, diarrhea, and odorous breath. Get a veterinarian. (Ordinary "strike anywhere" matches also contain phosphorus.)

Ethylene glycol: Radiator antifreeze contains this poison and is readily ingested by dogs. Induce vomiting at once, then give bicarbonate of soda.

Paint: Lead-base paint can cause lead poisoning, either when the liquid paint is swallowed or when excessive amounts of flaked paint are chewed from a painted surface. Symptoms include rapid breathing, restlessness, and collapse. Induce vomiting and give Epsom salts as an antidote

Pyrophosphates (Malathion, Parathion, Pestox, etc.): These are absorbed through the skin. Symptoms include pinpoint pupils, salivation, cramps, watery eyes, and muscular twitching. Bathe your dog with soap and water and get him to a veterinarian quickly.

Strychnine: The kind of poison people use to intentionally poison dogs or small rodents. Violent convulsions with the head and legs extended are a good sign of strychnine poisoning. *Do not induce vomiting.* Contact your vet immediately, and rush your dog to the hospital

If you know that your dog has eaten strychnine but symptoms have not yet begun, your vet may advise that you give your dog a sleeping capsule.

Warfarin: A common ingredient in rat poison. It is not supposed to harm dogs, but it sometimes does. The drug acts as an anticoagulant, causing death by internal bleeding. If your dog has eaten warfarin, take him to your vet for a shot that will cause the blood to coagulate. If you wait until symptoms appear, it may be too late.

Head study of Ch. Potterdale Privilege. Courtesy Mr. and Mrs. Lewis, England.

9 *Beardie Be Good*

THE PSYCHOLOGY OF TRAINING

Training is accomplished by teaching your dog to associate a verbal command or signal with an action. Once he makes this association, more complicated exercises can be easily taught.

The dog reacts much like a very young child; he will choose the path of least resistance, especially if it is reinforced by approval of his superiors. In the case of the dog, the natural pecking order is very pronounced, from the pack leader to the weakest member of the pack. In fact, only the most dominant animals are allowed to breed in the wild. The offspring are quickly relegated to their respective positions within the litter, and as they grow, they accept their placements within the adult community based upon their dominance and physical prowess. A submissive animal will not often challenge those above him in the pecking order, even if he could effectively do so. A dog's rolling onto his back is an indication of submissiveness in a particular situation. All dogs are dominant to some animals and submissive to others.

So it is with the domestic dog. However, if you want a successful relationship with your pet, you must establish yourself as a "pack leader" substitute. This allows you to have absolute authority in the eyes of your dog. This is especially important if you own a male Beardie, for if he feels that you are not assuming command, he will gladly challenge you for the position. You must know what you want the dog to do and decide on a reasonable approach to achieve those results. A Beardie is extremely intelligent and capable of acting independently; however, he has also been selected for reasonable submissiveness, which aids in trainability. Therefore, your dog will try to please you once he knows what you want.

The true pack leader is consistent, so you will get better results in your training if you behave predictably. A dozen halfhearted attempts at controlling a situation will never be respected, while a severe correction will only have to be given once. Always think before you react. If you are too emotional or inconsistent, your dog will become frustrated. Proper behavior for the Beardie conditioned by a particular stimulus must be reinforced by approval each time that it occurs if training is to be effective.

A dog's attention span is short, especially when he is a puppy. Therefore, he responds better to short, fast-paced training sessions. About ten- to fifteen-minute sessions either once or twice a day are best. Once you lose his attention, he is no longer able to learn, and you will find yourself vainly fighting with him. Also, if you ever lose your temper, the dog has won the battle. Stay cool, calm, authoritative, consistent, and worthy of your position as the pack leader. Do not underestimate your dog's ability; he will never overestimate yours.

TRAINING GUIDELINES

There are a few basic rules that apply to any form of training. Success is dependent upon careful attention to these details.

Be Consistent

Always use the same words for a particular command, and require the same response from your dog each and every time you use the words. Training is basically achieving a desirable conditioned response from your dog, and it takes repetition to condition him thoroughly. Eventually, his response to a particular command will become automatic.

Use Clear Commands

Keep your verbal commands short, make them distinguishable from other words, and give them in an authoritative (not loud) tone of voice. Allow a short but reasonable time for your dog to react. Say, "Dog, come," not, "There's a good boy, wouldn't you like to come here?" If you are casual or uncertain, your dog's response will show these same attitudes.

Use Plenty of Praise

Obviously, you should praise your dog whenever he obeys. Even more important is to praise him immediately after you have corrected an incorrect action. Praise is the only way for your dog to recognize acceptable behavior. He cannot understand your words, so make your tone of voice or your touch show approval. If your dog is really uncertain, a few food treats may reassure him. Never substitute food for praise—the incentive to work is much higher if your dog is doing it to please you.

Use Proper Equipment

Equipment does not need to be elaborate, but it must be functional. For most types of training, a medium-weight chain "choke" collar and a flat, six-foot-long leather or nylon leash are best. For herding or tracking, a fifty-foot "long line" (usually made of nylon webbing) is necessary. For tracking, the dog must also wear a properly fitted harness, and you will need a leather glove or wallet for him to find. Nylon choke collars or show leads may be used, or a light chain collar may be substituted for conformation showing of a well-trained dog or for leash-breaking a very young pup. Rolled leather

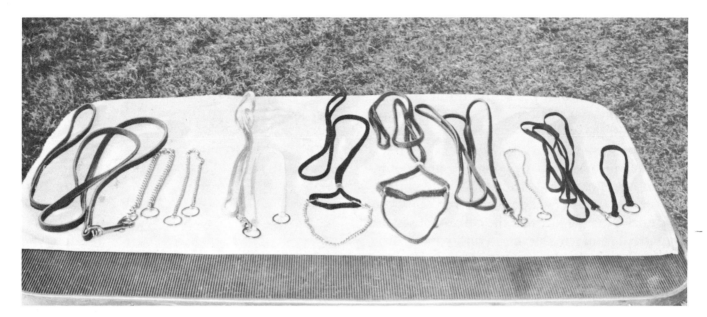

Above: Left to right: Obedience lead and collars, nylon choker and lead, two styles of martingales, fine choke chain and leather lead, and a nylon choker with web lead. The five styles on the right are suitable conformation leads.

Below: The correct way to put on a training collar.

collars are fine for yard wear and are a safety precaution while traveling. These are excellent for use in attaching ID tags, but they are unsuitable for training. Chain leashes are worthless, perhaps even harmful. They cut the handler's hands and hit the dog's face as he works. For this last reason, the metal snap on any lead should be reasonably small.

Use Aids Correctly

The choke collar must be put on the dog so that it tightens over the top of his neck when he is sitting at your left (*see* illustration). This allows the collar to release immediately after a jerk. If it is put on backward, the collar will remain tight, destroying its effectiveness as a training tool and perhaps choking the dog.

The lead should be held so that a slack loop appears at the collar. Fold the lead back and forth and hold the excess in your right hand. When you need to make a correction, quickly tighten and immediately release the pressure of the lead on the collar. Use a series of jerks if necessary, but never apply constant pressure to the collar.

When using a harness, keep your long line taut so that you can "read" your dog's responses to the track or livestock, but never allow a dog to lean into a collar. Correct him with quick jerks and praise. If you need a taut lead for any type of training, use the harness rather than the collar.

Never leave either a choke collar or a harness on a Beardie when you are not giving him a training lesson. He can easily hang himself if left unsupervised. Of lesser importance, but annoying nonetheless, is the fact that the collar will saw off the coat around the neck, leaving your Beardie with a short or bald area that can take months to grow back. If you must leave a collar on at all times, use a rolled leather or nylon collar.

Give Release Commands

Never leave your dog on a stay command without returning to release him. Many trainers use a separate command, "Wait," if they intend to give additional instructions. The dog is not allowed to move even one foot on a formal stay. By not returning to the dog, you teach him to break whenever he is tired of waiting. The dog cannot be blamed if you behave inconsistently in your demands on him.

When a lesson is finished, many trainers use "Okay" or "Free" to indicate that the session has ended and the dog is no longer expected to perform.

Encourage Your Dog to Challenge the Command

A dog that always performs perfectly does not truly know that he must respect the command. He has no idea that he'll be corrected, and therefore, he may be unreliable under a stressed condition. A dog that has lost a disagreement with the trainer over an exercise will be less likely to break later. Vary your training enough so that your dog respects the command in any situation. Distractions are vital in testing a

The proper heel position. Note how handler holds leash.

dog's training. The dog that will work only in a quiet, controlled environment is not really trained. He is only playing along because he has nothing better to do.

Vary Your Technique

If you experience continued problems with a specific exercise, go back to the beginning and retrain that exercise using a different approach that may be better suited to the individual dog. Seek professional advice if possible, or use some of the books listed in the bibliography for reference. Try to determine why your dog reacts as he does, and condition his responses accordingly.

TRAINING TIPS SPECIFIC TO BEARDIES

Beardies can be independent creatures. They are usually self-assured and sometimes strong willed. To train a Beardie successfully, you must establish yourself as the dominant personality so that your Beardie will respect you. Be consistent, but get tough if necessary to get his attention. Respect his intelligence, but demand his obedience. Use praise lavishly when he responds to you. You may think that he's hopeless at first, but after a couple of lessons, he will settle down and become much more manageable.

Beardies usually perform the worst on their "stay" exercises, which are taught first and require the dog to ignore distractions (nearly an impossibility for a Beardie on his first outing). Even if you are certain that your dog is the class dunce, keep working on this exercise (without losing your temper, or at least without letting your dog know that you've lost your temper) until he gives in. After that point, you will find him very quick to learn and rapidly passing his classmates in proficiency. The "stays" are very important for two reasons, so you must master them successfully. First, they establish your dominance over the dog, a condition that is mandatory for any further training. Secondly, the "stay" is fundamental to many future exercises that cannot be taught until the dog knows this step. It is the most useful tool in controlling your dog in everyday situations.

Beardies are very apt pupils, often learning their lessons as quickly as you demonstrate them. However, this same intelligence causes the dog to become easily bored and creatively defiant about performing by rote. You must work with enough speed and variety to keep your dog's interest, and whenever possible, show him a purpose for his actions. Alternate his lessons and create enough variations of each one to make them fun. You'll wind up with a better-trained dog that can perform all sorts of useful tasks.

WHAT EVERY BEARDIE SHOULD KNOW

A few basic concepts are necessary for every Beardie to learn for him to be socially acceptable. These are sometimes referred to as "yard manners" and constitute the very minimum of training that any conscientious owner should expect to do.

Training the dog to stand for examination.

Leash-Breaking

A young puppy can be started wearing a nylon choke collar or an English martingale. Older Beardies should be lead trained with a metal choke collar and leather leash. With the dog on your left side, start walking and encourage your dog to follow. Pat your leg and talk to him. This is not a formal "Heel," so don't use that command. If he follows along, stop after a few yards and pet him. Tell him how good he is, then resume walking. If he balks or runs the other way, give a snap on the lead, release the pressure immediately, and in a lighthearted voice encourage him to come with you. You may need to use several jerks in succession, each followed by praise.

Don't stop walking if your dog screams or throws himself; just ignore him and keep talking happily to him. Do not drag him along on a tight lead; rather, move him with a series of jerks and immediate releases of the collar. When he starts walking willingly, don't make him go too far at a time. A food treat may be offered to encourage him. If your dog forges ahead, jerk him back to your pace, but do not be too severe. Keep the lesson to about ten minutes and repeat once or twice a day until your dog trots along freely on a loose lead.

Sit and Lie Down

Give the verbal command "Sit," pull up on the collar, and push down on your dog's rear. As soon as he's sitting, praise him lavishly. Wait until he knows how to sit before you teach him to lie down. Start with him sitting. Say "Down," and step on his leash, forcing him quickly to the floor. Hold him until he quits struggling. If he resists, kneel beside him with one arm over his body and grasp one of his forelegs in each hand. Give the command "Down," and pull his legs toward you, moving your body into him and forcing him onto his side. Do this a few times, then return to stepping on the leash. Praise him immediately upon his response or your correction.

Stay

Sit your dog at your left side with the collar and leash on. Tell him to stay, and hold your open palm in front of his nose. Step in front of him and face him. If he moves, replace him and jerk up on the collar, repeating the command. Gradually increase the distance between you and your dog until you can walk across the room with him off lead. Always return and give a release command ("OK" or "Free") before allowing him to move.

Play is an important part of training. Ch. Walkoway's Frosted Flakes UD, HC, a BCCA HIT winner, "just having a ball." Owners: Linda and Jim Leek.

Not Jumping on People

Bump your dog's chest with your knee every time he jumps up, and say "No." This should discourage him if you are consistent and correct him *every* time. If you still have problems, grab your dog's front feet and run him backwards like a wheelbarrow. Flip him backward after about ten feet. Pretend that you're having a great time, and he'll soon decide that he doesn't like your game. Do not use the down command, because that should be used to tell your dog to lie down.

A big problem is that many dog-loving visitors will encourage your dog to jump up on them. By using a command such as "Feet" and pulling him off whenever he jumps on anyone, he can learn that jumping up is permitted unless specifically forbidden. If you are expecting visitors, put your Beardie on a leash and have him sit until the first excitement wears off.

Stop Biting

No dog should *ever* be allowed to bite unless he is badly injured and in shock. Stress or fear are not adequate excuses. Some Beardies tend to be "mouthy"—they nibble or grab with their mouths at every excuse. This must be discouraged. A slap on the muzzle and a sharp "No" may be adequate, but if your dog actually snaps, grab him and run your hand down his throat. This renders him unable to bite, but will gag and frighten him. Use your advantage to scold him and exert your dominance. Once your dog backs down, reassure him that you are still friends.

Come When Called

The biggest secret is to always praise your dog when he comes, regardless of how long it takes or what he has done. *Never* call him to you and punish him, or he will have second thoughts about coming the next time. He will think that he has been punished for coming and not connect the correction with any previous action. At three months of age, he will run away, but given another month to develop emotionally, he should come eagerly. Make sure that he trusts you and that you don't grab or frighten him every time he comes within reach. If your dog does not come willingly, he must be insecure about your reaction or motives. Loosen up, and so will your dog.

If your dog continually runs away, attach a long lead and correct him every time he fails to come when called. Follow the correction with a great deal of praise and reassurance.

Five-month-old future Ch. Chantilly High Stakes at Highlander, CGC, practicing the Come.

Coax the dog into show stance using bait.

The puppy should stand still, yet look alert.

SHOW TRAINING

Training a Beardie for conformation showing is simply a matter of keeping him under control. Most Beardies are cheerful extroverts and enjoy showing once they understand what is expected of them. Start training pups between ten weeks and five months of age. Puppies of this age are ready subjects and need to gain confidence in a show atmosphere before they enter adolescence. Keep training sessions short and fun, with a play period as a treat at the end. And remember to praise, praise, and praise.

The first thing that your puppy needs to learn is to trot freely on a loose lead. He should move in a straight line without weaving or crabbing. Use quick jerks and talk to him to bring him back in line. Speed up a bit to get your dog moving with his body in a straight line. When the pup has learned to move smoothly both in a straight line and as you circle the ring, practice making smooth turns (*see* gaiting patterns, Chapter 16) and walking smoothly into a stop as you face an imaginary "judge."

Your puppy must also learn to be friendly and relaxed while being examined by a stranger. Kneel beside your pup and hold his collar with your right hand, steadying him with your left hand resting under his flank. This way you can talk to the puppy and hold him while the judge examines him. Keep the training casual so that your puppy feels that it is a game. Do not worry at this point if he does not position his feet properly or if he does not stand still for more than a few seconds, and always give him plenty of praise.

Practice is required if you hope to obtain perfection. If a conformation training class is held in your area, make use of it. If not, or for additional exposure, take your puppy to shopping centers, parks, or wherever people congregate. Ask people to pet your puppy while you stack him. They will generally be happy to oblige if you explain what you are doing.

As the pup gains proficiency, begin "stacking" him for more control. Lift your puppy by the chest (*see* illustration) and set him down so that his front feet are positioned squarely and

naturally under his body. Hold him steady by placing your right hand under his chin. With your left hand, set his hind feet individually. Position them so that the metatarsus is vertical and slightly behind the line of the hip and about as far apart as the height of his hocks.

Some people continue to show adult dogs in this manner. However, it is most impressive if you can walk the dog into a natural stance and train him to stand squarely while he is "baited" to show expression. Of course, the dog must be constructed properly to be shown naturally, and many structural deficiencies can be minimized by clever stacking. Any knowledgeable judge is aware of this, however. Ch. Shiel's Mogador Silverleaf won a Best in Show because he was stepped forward several times at the judge's request and set himself up perfectly each time.

Right: A Beardie should gait freely on a loose lead.

Bottom Left: Lift the dog to set the front legs.

Bottom Right: Steady the puppy with a hand on his flank.

His closest competitor required constant stacking, and in the final evaluation, the handler had him slightly overstretched. A good Beardie with correct temperament looks better in a natural, alert pose than he does if artificially stacked.

CANINE GOOD CITIZENS

The Canine Good Citizen Test gives dog owners an opportunity to prove that their dog is a well-behaved member of society. It involves a non-competitive pass/fail test that demonstrates the dog's behavior in practical situations in the presence of unfamiliar people and other dogs. Your Beardie will be asked to accept a friendly stranger, walk on a loose lead, sit for petting, walk through a crowd, and respond to the commands Sit, Down, and Stay.

Local dog clubs and dog trainers offer the test. Watch your newspaper or ask a veterinarian or local pet-supply outlet for information. After he successfully completes the test, your Beardie will receive a certificate stating that he is a Canine Good Citizen. Some owners have found this helpful in obtaining rental housing that permits a dog, or admittance to public places where a dog might otherwise be prohibited.

OBEDIENCE TRAINING

Obedience training begins with the same exercises used to teach yard manners but demands more precise reactions and continues into more advanced work. Each exercise has practical applications, and there are three levels of proficiency, each level adding new and more difficult exercises (*see* Chapter 17). The first stage can earn a degree called the Companion Dog (CD), which is indeed descriptive. Any obedience-trained Beardie makes a superior pet, and obedience lessons are highly recommended for any dog. They will enhance your relationship with the dog and benefit him in nearly any capacity. Obedience-trained dogs are often welcomed where other dogs are not allowed.

Ch. Daybreak Storm at Candelaria, UD, HC demonstrates the high jump.

All obedience work is started with your dog in the heel position (sitting at your left with his front legs even with your legs). Once your dog is trained, hs is expected to perform with each command spoken only once. A dog that has been formally trained will work in a precise, efficient manner, which is exciting to watch.

Beardies are excellent workers as long as the routine is varied during training so that they do not get bored. Most Beardies enjoy advanced work if you can struggle through the initial stages of training. The sport of obedience is fun and constructive because it encourages individual achievement. Most communities offer training classes, at least on the beginning level. If you live where classes are not available, consult one of the many fine books on the subject. Be sure to work your dog where there are distractions so that he will be reliably trained for any situation.

OTHER ACTIVITIES FOR BEARDIES

Like other herding breeds, Bearded Collies are happiest when they have something to do. Obedience and show training are just a few of the activities in which Beardies successfully participate. Following are a few others you may wish to consider.

Agility

This exciting sport is rapidly becoming one of the most popular activities for dog owners. Anyone can do it, and Beardies, with their enthusiasm and high energy, are especially well suited to the sport. The agility course originated as a take-off on equestrian grand prix. The dog is required to navigate a series of obstacles and assorted hurdles. The course usually includes scaling an "A" frame, navigating both open and collapsible tunnels, crossing an elevated ramp, a seesaw or sway bridge, jumping, and a course of weave poles. Agility is a timed event that tests the willingness, athletic ability, and training of the dogs. The training also helps to mentally and physically prepare a dog for all types of work, and adds an element of freedom and fun that is lacking in structured obedience exercises.

Backpacking

While not a structured sport, you may find that you enjoy your Beardie's companionship more if

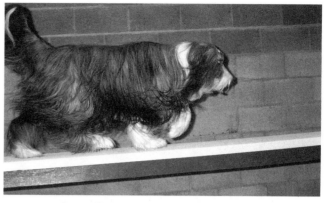

Ch. Walkoway's Frosted Flakes UD, HC crossing the ramp in agility.

you take him with you on camping and day hikes. Doggie backpacks are readily available, and it is easy to train a dog to carry a pack. Just be sure you start out slowly and build up his strength very gradually, and don't try it with your show dog — the pack may ruin his coat for showing. An adult Beardie can pack up to one-third of his body weight, which means he can easily carry his own food and supplies, plus some of yours. You'll be amazed at the bonding

Ch. Highlander Wildest Dreams HCT, CGC, in agility training with owner Beth Tilson.

that takes place when you share a wilderness adventure with him.

Flyball

This is another exciting spectator sport at which some Beardies excel. Teams of four dogs run in relay fashion over a course of jumps to a flyball box, where they must eject and catch the ball and retrieve it back over their jumps to their handler. The event is timed, with the fastest teams in a playoff for championship points. Obedience clubs often organize flyball teams, or you may find an unaffiliated group in your area.

"Catch that Flyball!" Courtesy of Alice Bixler.

Frisbee

Frisbee fetching is a perfect activity for the backyard, but it has also evolved into local, regional, and national competition. Besides being great exercise, your Beardie could win some impressive trophies.

Tracking

Tracking tests are held regularly in almost every location. Sponsored by AKC and UKC obedience and tracking clubs, they allow dogs to qualify for two different levels, Tracking Dog (TD) and Tracking Dog Excellent (TDX). The dog learns to rely on is natural scent discrimination and to work independently.

A tracking dog follows a scent along a track until it leads to a person or article bearing his scent. A well-trained dog can advance to search-and-rescue work or find your lost car keys in heavy underbrush. Either task is infinitely useful and satisfying and is within the reach of any Beardie owner who pursues training his dog to track. Several Beardies have competed in tracking, and the breed seems to excel at it.

A dog must be "certified" by a licensed tracking judge before he can enter a tracking test. The certification involves an informal test given to assure that the dog is qualified to compete. It helps to avoid unnecessary expense and time required to set up a test for dogs that are not ready. A great deal of space is needed, so most tracking tests limit the number of entries. The certification is usually somewhat easier than the actual tracking test, but individual

Jumping for a stick. Ch. Caldelaria Glengarry O'Riley CD, HC, owned by Laura Price and Judith M. LeRoy.

requirements are at the discretion of the judge. Only one tracking test must be successfully completed to obtain a TD.

Complete rules concerning tracking tests may be obtained by writing to the AKC. These rules are updated periodically, so it is wise to obtain a current set of regulations for either tracking or obedience before you start training. Professionally supervised classes in training a tracking dog are held in many areas of the country, or you can attempt training on your own with the help of a good book on the subject (*see* "Other Sources").

Service and Therapy Work

The ability of dogs to bring joy and companionship, as well as to assist, those in less fortunate situations knows no bounds. It takes a mature, somewhat quieter-natured Beardie to function in these roles, however. He must be trainable, intelligent, able to work independently, and have a certain degree of courage or boldness.

Therapy dogs visit the ill, handicapped, or those with learning disabilities. Because of their enthusiasm, Beardies may be too much for an elderly person, but they could excel with youth.

Service dogs assist people who are in wheelchairs, serve as hearing dogs for the deaf, or perform other helping tasks for the disabled.

Can./Am. Ch. Classical Mystique. Courtesy Brigette Nowak.

Ch. Highlander Spellbound HC, ROM, CGC.

Ch. Parcana Silverleaf Vandyke ROM.
Courtesy Mrs. Richard S. Parker.